Chares F. B Allnatt

Which is the True Church?

Or, a Few Plain Reasons for Joining the Roman Catholic Communion

Chares F. B Allnatt

Which is the True Church?

Or, a Few Plain Reasons for Joining the Roman Catholic Communion

ISBN/EAN: 9783337008048

Printed in Europe, USA, Canada, Australia, Japan

Cover: Foto ©Lupo / pixelio.de

More available books at **www.hansebooks.com**

WHICH IS THE TRUE CHURCH?

OR,

A Few Plain Reasons for Joining the Roman Catholic Communion.

BY

C. F. B. A.

St. Augustine, A.D. 400:—"Ye (Donatists) are not in the mountains of Sion, because you are not in *the City seated on a hill*, which has this sure mark, that it *cannot be hidden*. It is, therefore, known to all nations: now the party of Donatus is unknown to many nations: it is not, therefore, that city."—L. ii., *cont. Lit. Petilian.*, n. 239 (*al.* 104).

Origen, A.D. 210:—"We are not to give heed to those who say, *Behold, here is Christ*, but show Him not in the Church, which is filled with brightness from the East even unto the West; which is filled with true light, is *the pillar and ground of the truth*, in which as a whole is the whole advent of the Son of Man, who saith to all men, throughout the universe, '*Behold, I am with you all the days of life, even unto the consummation of the world.*'"—Tom. iii., *Com. in Matt.*, Tract. xxx. n. 46.

New Edition,

WITH AN ENLARGED APPENDIX AND ADDITIONAL NOTES.

EDINBURGH:

PRINTED AT THE BALLANTYNE PRESS.

1881.

St. Irenæus, Bishop of Lyons, A.D. 178 :—" In the Church God hath placed Apostles, Prophets, Doctors, and every other work of the Spirit, of which all they are not partakers who do not hasten to the Church, but by their evil sentiment and most flagrant conduct, defraud themselves of life. For where the Church is, there is the Spirit of God; and where the Spirit of God is, there is the Church and every grace : but the Spirit is truth."—*Adv. Hær.*, l. iii. c. 24, n. 2.

" He will judge all those who cause schisms ; men destitute of the love of God, and who have in view their own interest and not the oneness of the Church ; and who, on account of slight and exaggerated causes, rend and divide, and so far as in them lies, destroy the great and glorious Body of Christ ; men who have peace on their lips, but war in their actions ; who truly strain at a gnat, but swallow a camel. But no reformation can be effected by them so great as is the perniciousness of schism."—*Ib.*, l. iv. c. 33, n. 7.

PREFACE.

———

THE question which forms the title of this little work is one that must admit of very easy solution, seeing that the object, for which our Lord established His Church on earth, rendered it necessary that the MARKS—which were to distinguish her in all ages as the Divinely commissioned TEACHER OF THE NATIONS—should be plain and simple, and easily recognisable by those for whom His Religion itself was specially adapted and designed—the poor and ignorant, who constitute the great bulk of mankind.

Learned research, or anxious inquiry regarding the *doctrines* taught by the various and conflicting Christian communities, cannot be necessary for those who simply want to discover that Church which is the one unerring TEACHER appointed by God ; and the object of the following pages is to show, in as simple and brief a manner as possible, that the principal marks and characteristics of this Church, as plainly laid down in the Scriptures received by Protestants themselves, are, by a reference to notorious and acknowledged facts, and by the testimonies of Protestant or other hostile historians, whose works are accessible to all, so clearly shown to be recognisable in the Roman Catholic Church, and in her alone, as entirely to preclude the necessity for entering upon any of those irrelevant, tedious, and interminable controversies into which Protestant disputants are always desirous to draw off the attention of their readers.

The texts of Scripture are generally quoted from the Authorised Protestant Version ; and the historians (such as HALLAM, MILMAN, FROUDE, RANKE, NEANDER, GUIZOT, RENAN) or other authors, whose works have been freely cited in the Notes or Appendix, are all so well known for their strong Protestant or anti-Catholic sympathies, that whatever testimonies, at all favourable to the Catholic Church or religion in the past, may be found in their writings, will be acknowledged by all impartial persons to have a value, weight, and importance peculiar to themselves, and such as the statements of few other authors would in these days be likely to possess.

C. F. B. A.

WHICH IS THE TRUE CHURCH?

I. THE Object, for which the Redeemer established His Church or Kingdom on earth, was the conversion of the world to Christianity, the preservation and propagation of His One true Faith and Religion, Universally, in regard to Time and Place:—[1]

"I," He declared, "am 'the LIGHT OF THE WORLD. . . . For this cause came I into the world, that I should BEAR WITNESS UNTO THE TRUTH" (*John* iii. 17, viii. 12, xviii. 37. Comp. *Luke* ii. 32 ; *Acts* ii. 47, xiii. 47, xvii. 30 ; I *Tim.* ii. 4).

"Now is the judgment of this world : NOW SHALL THE PRINCE OF THIS WORLD BE CAST OUT.[2] And I, if I be lifted up from the earth, WILL

---

[1] The truth of this proposition is admitted by the ablest Protestant writers, *e.g.*, by Bishop PEARSON, in his *Commentary on the Apostles' Creed*, Art. ix., and by Bishop BUTLER, in his celebrated *Analogy of Religion*. The last-named writer says :—" In order to continue it (Christianity), and carry it on successively throughout all ages, a VISIBLE CHURCH was established. Had Christ and His Apostles only taught, and by miracles proved, religion to their contemporaries, the benefits of their instructions would have reached but to a small part of mankind. Christianity must have been in a great degree sunken and forgotten in a very few ages. To prevent this, appears to have been one reason why a Visible Church was instituted ; to be, like a city upon a hill, a standing memorial to the world of the duty which we owe our Maker ; to call men continually, both by example and instruction, to attend to it, and, by the form of religion ever before their eyes, remind them of the reality ; to be the repository of the oracles of God ; to hold up the light of revelation in aid to that of nature, and propagate it throughout all generations to the end of the world " (*Analogy*, Part ii. chap. i. sect. 7). And again :—" He founded a Church, to be to mankind a standing memorial of religion and invitation to it ; which He promised to be with always, even to the end " (*Ib.* chap. v. sect. 6).

[2] " Meaning," says the Anglican commentator BLOOMFIELD, "that now is the Prince of this world . . . about to be deposed from his rule, by the abolition of idolatry and superstition, and the introduction of true religion" (Note *in loc.*). "After the death of Christ the casting out *began*, and its first-fruits were the coming in of the Gentiles into the Church."—ALFORD (*in loc.*). Comp. *Rev.* xiv. 6–8.

DRAW ALL MEN UNTO MYSELF" (*John* xii. 31, 32. Comp. *Rom.* xvi. 20 ; *Rev.* xiv. 6–8).

"MANY shall come, from the East and West, and from the North and South, and shall sit down with Abraham, and Isaac, and Jacob IN THE KINGDOM OF HEAVEN.[1] But the children of the Kingdom [the unconverted Jews] shall be cast out into outer darkness" (*Matt.* viii. 11, 12 ; *Luke* xiii. 29. Comp. *Rom.* ix. 6–8, 24, x. 20, 21, xi. 12, 15, 25).

"The Kingdom of God IS COME UNTO YOU [JEWS]. . . . The Kingdom of God IS [ALREADY] AMONG YOU : . . . The Kingdom of God shall be taken from you, and GIVEN TO A NATION BRINGING FORTH THE FRUITS THEREOF" (*Matt.* xii. 28 ; *Luke* xvii. 21 ; *Matt.* xxi. 43. Comp. *Acts* xiii. 46, 47, xxviii. 28 ; *Rom.* x. and xi. ; Coloss. i. 6, 13 ; *Rom.* iv. 13, 16).

"Think not that I am come to destroy the Law or the Prophets : I am not come to destroy, but TO FULFIL. The Law and the Prophets were until John : SINCE THAT TIME THE KINGDOM OF GOD IS PREACHED, AND EVERY MAN PRESSETH INTO IT" (*Matt.* v. 17 ; *Luke* xvi. 16. Comp. *Matt.* xi. 11, 12).

"The Kingdom of Heaven is like to a GRAIN OF MUSTARD-SEED,[2] which a man took and sowed in his field : which indeed is the least of all seeds ; but when it is grown, it is the greatest among herbs, and BECOMETH A TREE, AND SHOOTETH OUT GREAT BRANCHES ; SO THAT THE BIRDS OF THE AIR COME AND LODGE UNDER THE SHADOW THEREOF. . . . The Kingdom of Heaven is like unto LEAVEN, which a

---

[1] Throughout the Gospels, the most common title given to the Visible Church of Christ is that of "THE KINGDOM OF HEAVEN" or "OF GOD ; "—a Kingdom, that is to say, "*not of this world*" (*John* xviii. 36), in its Origin and Object, but heavenly and divine. Besides the texts above quoted, see *Matt.* iii. 2 ; *Mark* i. 14 ; *Matt.* iv. 17, 23 ; *Luke* viii. 1 ; *Matt.* x. 7 ; *Luke* ix. 2, 11, 27, x. 9, xi. 20, xvii. 21 ; *Matt.* xxii. 2, xxv. 1, xiii. 11, 24, 41 ; *John* iii. 3, 5, &c.

[2] Dr. TRENCH, Protestant Archbishop of Dublin, says :—"His comparison of the growth of His Kingdom to that of a tree, must have been one with which many of His hearers were already familiar from the Scriptures of the Old Testament. The growth of a worldly kingdom had been set forth under this image (*Dan.* iv. 10–12 ; *Ezech.* xxxi. 3–9), that also of the Kingdom of God, (*Ezech.* xvii. 22–24 ; *Ps.* lxxx. 8). A mustard-seed is here chosen, . . . not with reference to its ultimate greatness, but to the proportion between the smallness of the seed and the greatness of the plant which unfolds itself therefrom. . . . What He desired to set before His disciples, was not merely that His Kingdom should be glorious, but that it should be glorious despite its weak, and slight, and despised beginnings. . . . In the birds flocking to the boughs of the mustard-tree when it had grown great, and there finding shelter and food, we are to recognise a prophecy of the refuge and defence that should be for all men in the Church : how that multitudes should hither resort, finding there protection from worldly oppression, as well as satisfaction for all the needs and wants of their souls" (*On the Parables*, pp. 105, 109, 6th edit.).

On the Parables of the LEAVEN and the NET, Dr. TRENCH says :—"The Parable of the Leaven is concerning the Kingdom of God, which 'cometh not

woman took, and hid in three measures of meal, UNTIL THE WHOLE WAS LEAVENED. . . . The Kingdom of Heaven is like unto a NET, that was cast into the sea, and GATHERED OF EVERY KIND" (*Matt.* xiii. 31–33, 47 ; *Mark* iv. 31, 32 ; *Luke* xiii. 19, 21).

"This gospel of the Kingdom SHALL BE PREACHED IN ALL THE WORLD, FOR A WITNESS UNTO ALL NATIONS [" FOR OBEDIENCE UNTO THE FAITH IN ALL NATIONS," *Rom.* i. 5], and then shall the end come" (*Matt.* xxiv. 14. Comp. *Rom.* xvi. 26 ; 1 *Cor.* xv. 24, 25).

"YE ARE THE LIGHT OF THE WORLD : A CITY THAT IS SET ON A HILL CANNOT BE HID" (*Matt.* v. 14. Comp. *Heb.* xii. 22 ; *Isai.* lx. 1, 3, 14).

"I have ordained you that ye should go and bring forth fruit, and THAT YOUR FRUIT SHOULD REMAIN" (*John* xv. 16. Comp. *Acts* xiii. 47, xxviii. 28 ; *Rom.* i. 13, xv. 9–19 ; *Coloss.* i. 6).

"THE SPIRIT OF TRUTH SHALL ABIDE WITH YOU FOR EVER : HE SHALL GUIDE YOU INTO ALL TRUTH" (*John* xiv. 17, xvi. 13).

"AS THE FATHER HATH SENT ME, EVEN SO SEND I YOU.[1] . . . ALL POWER IS GIVEN UNTO ME IN HEAVEN AND ON EARTH : GO YE, THERE-FORE, AND TEACH (MAKE DISCIPLES OF) ALL NATIONS ; BAPTIZING THEM IN THE NAME OF THE FATHER, AND OF THE SON, AND OF THE HOLY GHOST : TEACHING THEM TO OBSERVE ALL THINGS WHAT-SOEVER I HAVE COMMANDED YOU : AND LO ! I AM WITH YOU ALWAYS, EVEN UNTO THE END OF THE WORLD " (*John* xx. 21 ; *Matt.* xxviii. 18–20).

"Go ye into THE WHOLE WORLD, and PREACH THE GOSPEL[2] TO

with observation ;' this [of the mustard-seed] is concerning that same Kingdom, as it displays itself openly, and cannot be hid ; that declares the *intensive*, this the *extensive* development of the gospel. . . . They have, indeed, this in common, that they describe *the small and slight beginnings, the gradual progress, and the final marvellous increase of the Church*—or how, to use another image, the stone cut out without hands should become a great mountain, and fill the whole earth (*Dan.* ii. 34, 35). . . . This parable [of the *Net*] contains a pro-phecy of *the wide reach and potent operation of the gospel.* The kingdom of heaven should henceforth be a net cast into the broad stream of the whole world, and gathering or drawing together some out of every kindred, and tongue, and people, and nation " (*On the Parables*, pp. 104, 135).

[1] None have a right to PREACH without a lawful MISSION. "How," says St. Paul, "shall they preach, except they be *sent*?" (*Rom.* x. 15). Those who "assume this honour unto themselves" (*Heb.* v. 4) are guilty of the sin of Korah (see *Numb.* xvi. 3 *seq.; Jude* 11. Comp. *Jerem.* xxiii. 21). Our Lord Himself constantly appealed to His own Divine *Mission* (*John* vii. 16, 28, 29, xii. 44, 49, xvii. 3, &c.), which *Mission* He imparted to the Apostles (*Luke* x. 16 ; *John* xvii. 18, xx. 21), and the Apostles transmitted to their Successors — the whole Body of legitimate Pastors of the One true Church throughout all ages. (See *Acts* xiii. 2–4, xx. 28 ; 2 *Tim.* i. 6, 11, ii. 2 ; *Titus* i. 5 ; *Ephes.* iv. 11–13.)

[2] Thus was "the Prince of this world" to be deposed from his rule. He had "*seduced the whole world*" into idolatry (*Rev.* xii. 9) ; and therefore it was "*into

EVERY CREATURE. He that believeth, and is baptized, shall be saved; but he that believeth not, shall be condemned" (*Mark* xvi. 15, 16. Comp. *Rom.* x. 14–18).

"I will give UNTO THEE (PETER) THE KEYS" [the symbol of *Supreme Government.* Comp. *Isai.* xxii. 22, ix. 6; *Rev.* iii. 7] "OF THE KINGDOM OF HEAVEN; AND WHATSOEVER THOU SHALT BIND ON EARTH, SHALL BE BOUND IN HEAVEN; AND WHATSOEVER THOU SHALT LOOSE ON EARTH, IT SHALL BE LOOSED ALSO IN HEAVEN" (*Matt.* xvi. 19).

"I appoint unto YOU [My Apostles] a Kingdom, as My Father also hath appointed unto ME; that ye may eat and drink at My table in My Kingdom, and SIT ON THRONES, JUDGING THE TWELVE TRIBES OF ISRAEL"[1] (*Luke* xxii. 29, 30).

"Whatsoever YE shall bind on earth, shall be bound in heaven; and whatsoever YE shall loose on earth, shall be loosed in heaven" (*Matt.* xviii. 18).

---

the whole world" that the CHURCH of Christ was commanded to "*go;*" because it was through the instrumentality of that preaching, "by which faith cometh" (*Rom.* x. 14–17) that the Gentiles were to be "*turned from darkness unto light, from the power of Satan unto God,*" and to be "*translated into the Kingdom of His dear Son*" (*Acts* xxvi. 18; *Coloss.* i. 13).

By "*the world,*" the Empire of HEATHEN ROME (referred to by St. Luke as co-extensive with "*the whole world,*" *Luke* ii. 1) was specially signified. In *Rev.* xiii. 7, this Empire is spoken of as extending over "*all kindreds, and tongues, and nations*" ("*peoples, and multitudes, and nations, and tongues,*" *Rev.* xvii. 15); and upon its overthrow, and the establishment of the Church of Christ in its place, the Saints and Angels rejoice that "*the kingdoms of this world are become the Kingdom of the Lord and of His Christ*" (*Rev.* xi. 15). After this, Satan is said to be bound for a thousand years; *i.e.*, his power as "Prince of this world" has been broken by the fall of Paganism in the Roman Empire. He can no longer seduce the nations by making them worship idols.

With the words, "*Now shall the Prince of this world be cast out*" (*John* xii. 31), may be compared St. Paul's declaration to the Roman Church:—"The God of peace *shall bruise Satan under your feet shortly*" (*Rom.* xvi. 20). Both promises evidently referred to the overthrow of Paganism, and the near-at-hand conversion to Christianity of the great Heathen Empire of Rome (comp. *Rev.* xiv. 6–8).

The Protestant reader may refer to PALEY's *Evidences of Christianity*, part ii. ch. ix. sect. 1, for a short account of the rapid propagation of the Christian faith, and the conversion of the Empire under Constantine in the fourth century.

[1] "*The twelve tribes of Israel,*"—*i.e.*, the *spiritual* Israel, the whole Church,—converted Gentiles as well as converted Jews; the former being "*grafted in among*" the latter, and "*all baptized into one Body*" (*Rom.* xi. 17; 1 *Cor.* xii. 13; *Galat.* iii. 27–29; *Ephes.* iii. 6). Hence St. Paul calls the whole Christian Church "*the Israel of God*" (*Galat.* vi. 16), "*the commonwealth of Israel*" (*Ephes.* ii. 12),—declaring all—whether Jews or Gentiles—who had been "*baptized into Christ*" to be "*Abraham's seed, and heirs according to the promise*"

"Not for these only do I pray, but for them also who shall believe on Me through their word : THAT THEY ALL MAY BE ONE [BODY OR SOCIETY], IN ORDER THAT THE WORLD MAY BELIEVE THAT THOU HAST SENT ME ; . . . THAT THEY MAY BE MADE PERFECT IN ONE [ἵνα ὦσιν τετελειωμένοι εἰς ἕν—THAT THEY MAY BE PERFECTLY UNITED IN ONE BODY OR SOCIETY], AND THAT THE WORLD MAY [thereby] KNOW THAT THOU HAST SENT ME" (*John* xvii. 21, 22).

"He (Caiaphas) prophesied that Jesus should die for that nation ; and not for that nation only ; but that also HE SHOULD GATHER TOGETHER IN ONE [ἵνα συναγάγῃ εἰς ἕν,—THAT HE SHOULD COLLECT INTO ONE PEOPLE OR KINGDOM] THE CHILDREN OF GOD THAT WERE SCATTERED ABROAD" (*John* xi. 52).

"Other sheep [the Gentiles] I have, which are not of this Fold : them also I must bring [into it], and THEY SHALL HEAR MY VOICE ; AND THERE SHALL BE ONE FOLD AND ONE SHEPHERD" (*John* x. 16. Comp. *Acts* xiii. 47, xxviii. 28 ; *Ephes.* ii. 14 *seq.*, iii. 6).

"There is ONE BODY, and One Spirit, . . . One Lord, ONE FAITH, One Baptism. . . . And He gave some [to be] Apostles, . . . and some Pastors and Teachers ; FOR THE PERFECTING OF THE SAINTS, FOR THE WORK OF THE MINISTRY, FOR THE EDIFICATION OF THE BODY OF CHRIST ; UNTIL WE ALL COME INTO THE UNITY OF THE FAITH, AND OF THE KNOWLEDGE OF THE SON OF GOD, UNTO A PERFECT MAN ; . . . THAT HENCEFORTH WE BE NO MORE CHILDREN, TOSSED TO AND FRO, AND CARRIED ABOUT WITH EVERY WIND OF DOCTRINE, BY THE SLEIGHT OF MEN, AND CUNNING CRAFTINESS, WHEREBY THEY LIE IN WAIT TO DECEIVE ; BUT SPEAKING THE TRUTH [ἀληθεύοντες—maintaining and professing the true faith] IN CHARITY, MAY GROW UP INTO HIM IN ALL THINGS, WHICH IS THE HEAD, EVEN CHRIST" (*Ephes.* iv. 4, 5, 11-15).

"Christ is the Head of THE CHURCH ; and He is the Saviour of THE BODY, . . . HIS BODY, WHICH IS THE CHURCH" (*Ephes.* v. 23 ; *Coloss.* i. 24).

"We are ALL BAPTIZED INTO ONE BODY,[1] whether Jews or Gentiles,

(*Rom.* ix. 8, 24, iv. 11, 16 ; *Galat.* iii. 7, 9, 29). St. Peter, in like manner, applies to the whole body of the faithful the very titles that had formerly been given to the Jewish people ; calling them "*a chosen generation, a royal priesthood, an holy nation, a peculiar people ; that they should show forth the praises of Him who had called them out of darkness into His marvellous light*" (*Exod.* xix. 5, 6 ; I *Pet.* ii. 9. Comp. *Ephes.* ii. 19, 21 ; *Heb.* xii. 22, 28).

[1] That the *Visible* Church is signified under the title of "Body of Christ" is evident from the fact that, 1st, all THE BAPTIZED become members of it (I *Cor.* xii. 13. Comp. *Acts* ii. 41, 47) ; 2dly, these members have a "necessary" dependence on one another and on the whole body ; they perform various outward and visible functions (*Rom.* xii. 4-8), and hold external as well as internal communion ; so that "*when one member suffers, all the members suffer with it, or one member be honoured, all the members rejoice with it*" (I Cor. xii. 15-26). 3dly, St. Paul speaks of the reception of the EUCHARIST as a necessary bond and evidence of

whether bond or free ; " and " God hath tempered the Body together, . . . THAT THERE SHOULD BE NO SCHISM IN THE BODY. . . . For as the [natural] body is one, and hath many members, and all the members of that one body, being many, are one body ; so also is Christ. . . . Now ye are the Body of Christ, and members in particular; . . . MANY MEMBERS, YET BUT ONE BODY. . . . IS CHRIST DIVIDED ? " (1 *Cor.* xii. 12, 13, 20, 24, 25, 27, i. 13. Comp. *Rom.* xii. 4, 5 ; *Ephes.* ii. 14, 15, iii. 6, &c.).

" THE CHURCH OF THE LIVING GOD [is] THE PILLAR AND FOUNDA-TION OF THE TRUTH " [1] (1 *Tim.* iii. 15).

" Unto Him be glory IN THE CHURCH, by Jesus Christ, throughout all ages, world without end " (*Ephes.* iii. 21).

" Thou art PETER (Chipha), and UPON THIS ROCK (Chipha) I WILL BUILD MY CHURCH, AND THE GATES OF HELL [Πύλαι ᾅδου—the Powers of Darkness,—Satan and his hosts] SHALL NOT PREVAIL AGAINST IT. And unto thee will I give the Keys of the Kingdom of Heaven," &c. (*Matt.* xvi. 17, 18).

" HE THAT HEARETH YOU, HEARETH ME ; and he that despiseth YOU, despiseth ME, and he that despiseth ME, despiseth Him that sent ME" (*Luke* x. 16).

" If he neglect to HEAR THE CHURCH, let him be unto thee as an heathen man and a publican. Verily I say unto you : WHATSOEVER

---

membership : " We, being many, are One Bread, One Body, *because we all partake of that One Bread*" (1 *Cor.* x. 17). Lastly, because the whole Body is said to be "*edified*" or "*built up*" through the instrumentality of that visible hierarchy and ministry which Christ has set over it for that express purpose.

[1] See the notes on this text in the Greek Testaments edited by BLOOMFIELD and ALFORD. The former says that the attempt made by some Protestant controversialists to refer the words "pillar and foundation of the truth" to what *follows* "lies open to *insuperable objections*, as stated by Poole, Benson, and Scott." ALFORD says : " If a sentence like this occurred in the Epistle, I should feel it a weightier argument against its genuineness than any which its opponents have yet adduced."

To the interpretation (devised by other Protestant controversialists) which refers the words to *Timothy*, Dean ALFORD says : " To the sentence thus arranged and understood there are weighty and, I conceive, *fatal objections*." BLOOMFIELD says : " The natural connection of the words is certainly *not*, as some imagine, to Timothy ; for that would be an utter violation of the construction, and involve somewhat of an incongruity. . . . There can be no doubt but that the true reference is to ἥτις ἐστὶν ἐκκλησία [" *which is the Church*," &c.], as was maintained by almost all the ancient expositors and many eminent Protestant commentators, as Grotius, Bishop Hall, Calvin, Hammond, Gothofred, Weber, Schmid, Deyling, Whitby, Macknight, and Bishop Van Mildert ; and of the recent expositors, Dr. Peile ; and of the foreign, Wiesing, Huther, and Mack, who understand it of *the Church universal, administered under an external form of government, and which, by maintaining the revelation of God and His religion, upholds it as a foundation does a building, or as pillars support an edifice. . . . Any other mode of explanation is, both philologically and otherwise, quite untenable*" (note *in loc.*).

YE shall bind on earth shall be bound in heaven," &c. (*Matt.* xviii. 17, 18).

" He that despiseth, despiseth NOT MAN, BUT GOD" (1 *Thess.* iv. 8. Comp. *ch.* ii. 13).

" WE are of God : HE THAT KNOWETH GOD, HEARETH US ; he that is not of God, heareth us not. HEREBY KNOW WE THE SPIRIT OF TRUTH, AND THE SPIRIT OF ERROR" (1 *John* iv. 6).

(See also *Acts* ii. 42, 47, xv. 6, 28, xvi. 4, xx. 28, 30; *Rom.* xvi. 17; 1 *Cor.* i. 10, xi. 16; *Heb.* xiii. 7, 9, 17; *Galat.* i. 9; 1 *Tim.* i. 3, 20; 2 *Tim.* ii. 17, 18; *Titus* i. 10, 11, iii. 10, 11, &c.)

With these declarations of our Lord and His Apostles should be compared the following and similar prophecies of the Old Testament :—

" In thee shall ALL THE NATIONS OF THE EARTH BE BLESSED. . . . And thy seed shall be as the dust of the earth ; and thou shalt spread abroad to the West, and to the East, and to the North, and to the South ; and IN THEE AND IN THY SEED SHALL ALL THE FAMILIES OF THE EARTH BE BLESSED" (*Gen.* xii. 3, xxii. 18, xxviii. 14. Comp. *Rom.* iv. 11–17, ix. 8, 24; *Galat.* iii. 7–9, 26–29; *Ephes.* iii. 6; *Matt.* viii. 11; *Luke* xiii. 29.

" The sceptre shall not depart from Judah, nor a lawgiver from between his feet, until SHILOH come, and UNTO HIM SHALL THE GATHERING OF THE PEOPLE BE" (*Gen.* xlix. 10. Comp. *John* xi. 52, xii. 32).

" Yet have I set My King upon My holy hill of Zion. . . . Ask of Me, and I shall give thee THE HEATHEN FOR THY INHERITANCE, AND THE UTTERMOST PARTS OF THE EARTH FOR·THY POSSESSION. Thou shalt break them with a rod of iron ; thou shalt dash them in pieces like a potter's vessel" (*Psalm* ii. 6–9). This prophecy is applied to the MESSIAS in *Acts* iv. 25, xiii. 32, 33; *Heb.* i. 5, v. 5; *Rev.* ii. 27, xii. 5, xix. 15.

" He shall have DOMINION ALSO FROM SEA TO SEA, AND FROM THE RIVER UNTO THE ENDS OF THE EARTH. . . . ALL KINGS SHALL FALL DOWN BEFORE HIM ; ALL NATIONS SHALL SERVE HIM" (*Psalm* lxxii. 8, 9. Comp. *Zech.* ix. 9, 10; *Matt.* xxi. 41 *seq.*). See also *Psalm* cx. (comp. *Matt.* xxii. 43-45 ; *Acts* ii. 34-36 ; 1 *Cor.* xv. 25 ; *Heb.* v. 6).

" And the STONE that smote the image BECAME A GREAT MOUNTAIN, AND FILLED THE WHOLE EARTH. . . . And in the days of these kings [of the Roman Empire] shall the God of heaven set up A KINGDOM WHICH SHALL NEVER BE DESTROYED : AND . . . IT SHALL STAND FOR EVER" (*Dan.* ii. 35, 44; *Luke* i. 33; *Heb.* xii. 28).

" And it shall come to pass in the last days,[1] that THE MOUNTAIN OF THE LORD'S HOUSE SHALL BE ESTABLISHED IN THE TOP OF THE MOUN-

---

[1] " *The last days*," *i.e.*, in the present Christian Dispensation. See *Acts* ii. 16, 17 ; *Heb.* i. 2 ; 1 *Cor.* x. 11 ; 1 *Pet.* i. 20. Comp. *Ephes.* i. 10 ; *Galat.* iv. 4 (" *the fulness of times*").

TAINS, AND SHALL BE EXALTED ABOVE THE HILLS, AND ALL NATIONS SHALL FLOW UNTO IT. Aηd many people shall go and say, Come ye, and let us go up to the mountain of the Lord, to the House of the God of Jacob : and He will teach us of His ways, and we will walk in His paths : for out of Zion shall go forth the law, and the word of the Lord from Jerusalem "[1] (*Isai.* ii. 2, 3 ; *Micah* iv. 1, 2). The early Fathers were unanimous in interpreting these texts of the CHURCH of CHRIST,—as also are the most learned Protestant commentators, such as Stanhope, Mant, Michaelis, Lowth, Clarke, Scott, Patrick, Henderson, &c.

" The people that walked in darkness have seen a great light. . . . For unto us a child is born, unto us a son is given, and the government shall be upon his shoulder : . . . OF THE INCREASE OF HIS GOVERNMENT AND PEACE THERE SHALL BE NO END," &c. (*Isai.* ix. 2, 6, 7. Comp. *Matt.* iv. 14–17 ; *Luke* i. 32, 33, 79, ii. 32).

"AND THINE EYES SHALL SEE THY TEACHERS : AND THINE EARS SHALL HEAR A VOICE BEHIND THEE SAYING, THIS IS THE WAY, WALK YE IN IT, WHEN YE TURN TO THE RIGHT HAND, AND WHEN YE TURN TO THE LEFT " (*Isai.* xxx. 21). See also *Isai.* xxxv. 4–8, xl. 3–11 (comp. *Matt.* iii. 3 ; *Luke* i. 76, iii. 3–6) ; *Isai.* xlii. 1 *seq.* (comp. *Matt.* xii. 17–21).

"And He said, It is a light thing that thou [the MESSIAS] shouldest be My servant to raise up the tribes of Jacob, and to restore the preserved of Israel ; I will also give thee for A LIGHT TO THE GENTILES, THAT THOU MAYEST BE MY SALVATION UNTO THE ENDS OF THE EARTH. . . . Kings shall see and arise, princes also shall worship. . . . The children which thou [ZION—THE CHURCH] shall have shall say, The place is too strait for me : give place to me that I may dwell. . . . Thus saith the Lord God, Behold I will lift up mine hand to the GENTILES, and set up my standard to the people : and they shall bring thy sons in their arms, and thy daughters shall be carried upon their shoulders. AND KINGS SHALL BE THY NURSING FATHERS, AND THEIR QUEENS THY NURSING MOTHERS : THEY SHALL BOW DOWN TO THEE WITH THEIR FACE TOWARD THE EARTH, AND LICK UP THE DUST OF THY FEET " (*Isai.* xlix. 6, 7, 20–23. Comp. *Acts* xiii. 47 ; *Luke* ii. 32 ; *Rom.* xi. 12, 15, 25, xv. 9, 12, 21). See also *Isai.* lii. 1, 7, 10, 13–15. Comp. *Rom.* x. 15, xv. 21 ; *Luke* iii. 6).

" Sing, O barren,[2] thou that didst not bear. . . . Enlarge the place of

---

[1] " *Out of Zion,*" &c. Comp. *Luke* xxiv. 47. " Zion " and " Jerusalem " are, however, the titles of the Christian Church. See *Galat.* iv. 26 ; *Heb.* xii. 22. To the objection that the *peace* so vividly described in *Isai.* ii. 4, has not existed in the present dispensation, it may be replied, 1*st,* that the language is highly figurative ; 2*dly,* that still stronger expressions are used to describe the " peace " spoken of in ch. xi. 6–10, as existing under the Messias (comp. *Acts* xiii. 23 ; *Rom.* xv. 12) ; and, as HENDERSON admits, " with regard to the application of *this* prophecy to the Messiah, a greater degree of unanimity obtains among interpreters than in reference to almost any other."

[2] In most of the ancient prophecies which refer to the Christian Church or Dispensation, the Messias is spoken of as continuing and prolonging the Old

thy tent, and let them stretch forth the curtains of thine habitations : spare not ; lengthen thy cords, and strengthen thy stakes : For THOU SHALT BREAK FORTH ON THE RIGHT HAND AND ON THE LEFT ; AND THY SEED SHALL INHERIT THE GENTILES, AND MAKE THE DESOLATE CITIES TO BE INHABITED. . . . AS I HAVE SWORN THAT THE WATERS OF NOAH SHOULD NO MORE GO OVER THE EARTH ; SO HAVE I SWORN THAT I WOULD NOT BE WROTH WITH THEE, NOR REBUKE THEE. FOR THE MOUNTAINS SHALL DEPART, AND THE HILLS BE REMOVED ; BUT THY KINDNESS SHALL NOT DEPART FROM THEE, NEITHER SHALL THE COVE-NANT OF MY PEACE BE REMOVED, SAITH THE LORD THAT HATH MERCY ON THEE. . . . ALL THY CHILDREN SHALL BE TAUGHT OF THE LORD, AND GREAT SHALL BE THE PEACE OF THY CHILDREN. . . . NO WEAPON THAT IS FORMED AGAINST THEE SHALL PROSPER ; AND EVERY TONGUE THAT SHALL ARISE IN JUDGMENT AGAINST THEE, THOU SHALT CONDEMN" (*Isai.* liv. 1, 2, 3, 9, 10, 17). This prophecy is expressly applied to the Christian Church by St. Paul in *Galat.* iv. 22–31. Comp. *Rom.* ix. 24–26.

"And the Redeemer shall come to Zion. . . . As for Me, this is MY COVENANT with them, saith the Lord : MY SPIRIT THAT IS UPON THEE, AND MY WORDS WHICH I HAVE PUT IN THY MOUTH, SHALL NOT DEPART OUT OF THY MOUTH, NOR OUT OF THE MOUTH OF THY SEED, NOR OUT OF THE MOUTH OF THY SEED'S SEED, SAITH THE LORD, FROM HENCE-FORTH AND FOR EVER" (*Isai.* lix. 20, 21. Comp. *Jerem.* xxxi. 31–34 ; cited by St. Paul in *Heb.* viii. 7–13).

"The GENTILES shall come to thy light, and kings to the brightness of thy rising : . . . the abundance of the sea shall be converted unto thee, the forces of the Gentiles shall come unto thee. . . . THY GATES SHALL BE OPEN CONTINUALLY ; THEY SHALL NOT BE SHUT DAY NOR NIGHT ; THAT MEN MAY BRING UNTO THEE THE FORCES OF THE GENTILES, AND

Economy ; the Christian Polity being described, not as something antagonistic to or different from that which then existed, viz., the Jewish, but rather as its transformation, perfection, and development. *The future Church of the Gentiles is identified with the Jewish Church then existing;* and the prophecies relating to the establishment and increase of the Church of the Messias are addressed to her in her imperfect, "barren," and undeveloped state, confined and limited as she then was to one small nation and people.

Many of these prophecies were declared by our Lord or His Apostles to have received, or to be about to receive, their fulfilment by the establishment or increase of the Christian or Gentile Church (see *Matt.* iii. 2, 3, iv. 16, 17, v. 17, viii. 11, xi. 3, 4, 12–14, xii. 17–21, 28, xxi. 4–15, 43 ; *Luke* ii. 32, iv. 18–21, vii. 27, 28, xi. 20, xvi. 16, xvii. 21 ; *Acts* ii. 16–36, xiii. 23, 32, 33, 47, xv. 14–17 ; *Rom.* iv. 16, ix. 8, 24, 25, x. 20, xi. 12, 15, 25, xv. 9, 12, 21, xvi. 26 ; *Galat.* iii. 7, 9, 14, 16, 26–29, iv. 26–31 ; *Ephes.* ii. 12, iii. 6; *Heb.* viii. 6–12, x. 16, xii. 22, 28, &c.) ; and, from the earliest ages, all the great Christian Apologists unhesitatingly appealed to their actual fulfilment in the present Dispensation, as being one of the most luminous evidences of the Divine mission of Christ and of the Church which He established.

THAT THEIR KINGS MAY BE BROUGHT. FOR THE NATION AND KING-
DOM THAT WILL NOT SERVE THEE SHALL PERISH. . . . The sons also of
them that afflicted thee shall come bending unto thee; and all they that
despised thee shall bow themselves down at the soles of thy feet; and
they shall call thee, THE CITY OF THE LORD, THE ZION OF THE HOLY
ONE OF ISRAEL" (*Isai.* lx. 3, 5, 11, 14. Comp. vers. 1, 2, with *Matt.*
iv. 16, 17; ver. 14 with *Heb.* xii. 22, *Matt.* v. 14; and ver. 5 *seq.* with
Rom. xi. 12, 15, 25, &c). See also *Isai.* lxi. (Comp. *Luke* iv. 17–21);
Isai. lxii. 1–7, 11, 12, lxv. 1 *seq.* (Comp. *Rom.* x. 20, ix. 24, 30.)
¡ "FROM THE RISING OF THE SUN, EVEN TO THE GOING DOWN OF THE
SAME, MY NAME SHALL BE GREAT AMONG THE GENTILES, and IN EVERY
PLACE incense shall be offered to My name, and a pure offering; for My
name shall be great among the heathen, saith the Lord of hosts" (*Mal.*
i. 11. Comp. *Rom.* xv. 16).

II. From the passages of Scripture above cited it is also
evident that, in order to secure and effect the unfailing preservation and world-wide propagation of His true Faith and
Religion, that CHURCH or TEACHING BODY, which the
Redeemer appointed to be the Organ and Instrument of its
preservation and extension, must, among the characteristics
and prerogatives which are essential to it, possess—

(1.) PERPETUAL VISIBILITY;

(2.) APOSTOLICITY—the ORDERS AND MISSION OF ITS
PASTORS, as well as its DOCTRINE and WHOLE POLITY,
being transmitted through continuous and legitimate SUC-
CESSION FROM THE APOSTLES;

(3.) CATHOLICITY—or UNIVERSALITY as to TIME (or
DURATION), PLACE (or EXTENT), and DOCTRINE;

(4.) UNITY—in its FAITH, SACRAMENTS, PUBLIC WOR-
SHIP, and GOVERNMENT;

(5.) INFALLIBILITY—or INERRANCY IN ITS TEACHING;
which five marks and prerogatives of the true Church may,
for the purpose of this argument, be mainly reduced to *two*
only, viz., CATHOLICITY and UNITY; it being sufficient to
observe that the Church must have been endowed, in the first
place, with a THREEFOLD CATHOLICITY—

(1.) of TIME or DURATION,

(2.) of PLACE or EXTENT,

(3.) of DOCTRINE,

in order to fulfil the great Commission given to her by her Divine Founder, viz., to TEACH—

(1.) "ALWAYS, TO THE END OF THE WORLD," or "UNTIL WE ALL COME INTO THE UNITY OF THE FAITH" (Catholicity of TIME);

(2.) To "ALL NATIONS," and "EVERY CREATURE" (Catholicity of PLACE, or EXTENT);[1]

(3.) "ALL THINGS WHATSOEVER" her Lord had "COMMANDED," "ALL TRUTH" (Catholicity of DOCTRINE);
and, in the second place, that this Church must be so essentially and organically "ONE"—("ONE FOLD," "ONE BODY," ONE "KINGDOM," "CITY," or "HOUSE," that CANNOT BE "DIVIDED AGAINST ITSELF");[2] and, throughout her whole domain, and in every age, must so *visibly manifest* her Divinely-secured Unity—

(1.) of FAITH, or DOCTRINAL TEACHING and BELIEF,
(2.) of COMMUNION,
(3.) of REGIMEN or GOVERNMENT,

[1] When St. Paul, in his Epistle to the ROMANS, speaks of the Church as receiving "THE FULNESS OF THE GENTILES," and causing the reconciliation of "THE WORLD" by her preaching of the Gospel (see *Rom.* i. 5, 8, x. 14-17, xi. 12, 15, 25, xv. 12, 18, xvi. 26, &c.), could any doubt that the fulfilment of such prophecies as *Isai.* liv., lx., *Mal.* i. 11, was shortly to be effected through her instrumentality? Or, when again—writing to the same Church of Rome, he said that God "WOULD BRUISE SATAN UNDER THEIR FEET SHORTLY" (*Rom.* xvi. 20)—evidently referring to the ancient prophecy that "*the Seed of the woman should bruise the Serpent's head*" (*Gen.* iii. 15), and to our Lord's declaration that He was about to "*cast out the Prince of this world, and to draw all men unto Himself*"—could he have meant anything else than that that great City, which was then the head and centre of Pagan idolatry—"the mother of harlots and abominations of the earth" (*Rev.* xvii. 5)—should shortly become the head and centre of the true religion, the mother of all Churches, and mainspring of the propagation of Christianity through the entire world?

[2] The very titles of "KINGDOM," "CITY," and "HOUSE," so often given to the Church in Scripture (see the texts above quoted ; especially *Isai.* ii. 2, lx. 14, lxii. 12; *Dan.* ii. 44; *Heb.* xii. 28; *Matt.* v. 14; *Ephes.* ii. 21; *Coloss.* i. 13; I *Tim.* iii. 15; 2 *Tim.* ii. 20; *Heb.* iii. 6, x. 21, xii. 22; I *Pet.* ii. 5, iv. 17, &c.), when taken in connection with the promises of her *perpetuity*, necessarily imply her absolute and organic UNITY : for "*Every Kingdom, divided against itself, is brought to desolation ; and every city or house, divided against itself, will not stand*" (*Matt.* xii. 25). On ONE ROCK was this Church built ; to ONE were the "Keys" —the symbol of supreme power, the mastership over the Lord's House, the guardianship of the Lord's City—committed ; to ONE was the Pastorship of the whole Flock delegated (*John* xxi. 15-17); in order that the UNITY of the same might be both manifested and secured.

as not only to present to the unbelieving "WORLD" (*John* xvii. 21, 23; *Rom.* i. 8, xi. 15; *Coloss.* i. 6) a plain token and evidence of the Divine Mission of her Founder, but also to guarantee to her own faithful children, and to all seekers after the Truth, entire exemption from and security against the vain and ever-varying speculations of all mere human teachers and heretical innovators.

III. Hence it necessarily follows: that no Church or body of professing Christians can claim or pretend to be THE TRUE CHURCH OF JESUS CHRIST, which cannot prove itself—

(1.) To have had a VISIBLE EXISTENCE IN ALL AGES FROM THE TIME OF CHRIST;

(2.) To have been CONTINUALLY ENGAGED IN FULFILLING, through a Ministry duly ordained and "*sent,*" the Commission given to it by Christ,—by "DISCIPLING AND BAPTIZING," and thus progressively extending her dominion over "ALL NATIONS" of the world;

(3.) Teaching them the WHOLE[1] Revelation of Jesus Christ,

---

[1] But not, of course, always and everywhere with the same explicitness and fulness (see 1 *Cor.* iii. 1, 2; *Heb.* v. 11-14). It is well known that, during several centuries, the Canon of Scripture itself remained undetermined; and Protestants themselves will hardly deny that the Nicene Creed contained a *development* of the doctrine contained in that of the Apostles, or that the Athanasian Creed contained a still further development or explication of the Christian Faith regarding the Holy Trinity and the Incarnation.

"There has ever been," says Dr. W. TODD, "and there is still, a gradual and very striking growth of Christian doctrine in the Church. Truths which were once held in their naked simplicity have unfolded, by a necessary development, more and more of the profound mysteries contained within each of them. As time goes on, the Christian intellect, leaning upon the support of the Church, is enabled to see more clearly the bearing of one doctrine upon another, its relation to truths that flow out of it, its place in the analogy of the faith, its full scope and significance. Dogmas, in some sense new, spring out of more general truths,—new because hitherto only faintly perceived, though in germ and in substance they have always been in the revelation of Christ. All theologians admit a progression of doctrine in the Church; and unless Christianity be nothing more than a bare and dry code of laws, there must be some such progression. Every truth that comes from God must contain within itself unsearchable treasures of wisdom. It is like a seed sown in the earth, which grows and spreads into a large tree. *But this growth is only in the Church.* Outside, truth is questioned, doubted, torn in pieces, tossed about by every vain blast. Within, there is a consistent and true growth. And everything favours this growth—the meditations of the devout, the inquiries of the learned, nay, the very contradictions of the heretics. For the greater part of the

and instructing them in "ALL" His Doctrines, Precepts, and Ordinances ;

(4.) Always and everywhere so manifesting herself as "ONE,"—in her Faith, Public Worship, Sacraments, and Government,—as to present to the whole world a proof of her Divine Origin, and of her being in possession of an unerring Teaching Authority, such as must at all times bring those who submit to it to "*meet in the unity of the faith*," and preserve them from being carried about by the various blasts of false doctrine, to which those outside the pale of the true Church are continually exposed.

IV. Now, no PROTESTANT Church—*i.e.*, no Church out of communion with, or teaching doctrines opposed to, the Roman Catholic Church—was, or ever pretended to have been, thus VISIBLE, APOSTOLIC, CATHOLIC, and ONE, either before or subsequently to the time of the so-called "Reformation."

It was not by any such Church,[1] it was not by any of

---

decrees of Councils and decisions of the Holy See have originated in the necessity of guarding the faithful against the false opinions put forth by those who are separated from the Church. In this way, even the attempt to sow discord and to bring in false doctrine has only tended to the completion and perfection of Catholic doctrine" (*Lect. on the Inspiration and Interpretation of Holy Scripture*, 1863, p. 66). See also *The Written Word*, by the Rev. W. HUMPHREY, 1877, pp. 199-206. Cardinal NEWMAN'S remark, that "the growth or development in the Church's teaching *proceeds on fixed laws, under the safeguard of her infallibility, which secures her from whatever is abnormal or unhealthy*," is alone enough to show the futility of the ordinary Protestant objections in regard to it.

The principle of *development* of Christian doctrine is admitted by the Anglican Bishop BUTLER, who remarks that "it is not at all incredible that a book [the Bible], which has been so long in the possession of mankind, should contain many truths as yet undiscovered," and that "possibly it might be intended *that events as they come to pass should open and ascertain the meaning of several parts of Scripture*" (*Analogy*, pt. ii. ch. iii. sect. 9).

[1] Some Protestants are still fond of referring to the miserable hole-and-corner sects of the Middle Ages,—the ALBIGENSES, WALDENSES, CATHARISTS, &c., —as having promulgated in their day some doctrines akin to those of modern sectaries ; but the true history of the origin, doctrines, and principles of those "precursors of the Reformation" has been thoroughly exposed during the last half-century by candid Protestant writers,—such as HALLAM (*Middle Ages*, ch. ix.), MAITLAND (*Facts and Documents illustrative of the History, Doctrines, and Rites of the Ancient Albigenses and Waldenses*, 1832 ; and *Letter to Dr. Mill, containing Strictures on Mr. Faber's Work, &c.*, 1839), and TODD (*Discourses on the*

the sects of Protestantism, either separately or collectively, it was not by any of their "Bible" or "Missionary" societies that the Commission given by Christ to "DISCIPLE AND BAPTIZE ALL NATIONS," was in every or in *any* former age

Prophecies relating to Antichrist, Donnellan Lectures in Trin. Coll., Dublin, 1840, *notes*, pp. 399-453. See also NEANDER'S *Church Hist.*, Bohn's edit., vol. viii. pp. 283 *seq.*, 295-331, 350 *seq.*; BLUNT'S *Dict. of Sects*, &c.; and a valuable work entitled *Origines Protestantica, or Suggestions for an Historical Inquiry into the Origin of the Protestant Religion*, Longhurst, Lond., 1877); and what Protestants are really called upon to do is to show, if they can, some other Church than the Catholic which has fulfilled Christ's commission by "*teaching and baptizing all nations*,"—some other Church which has been in all ages "*the Light of the world*," "*the Pillar and Foundation of the Truth*," "*the City set on a hill which could not be hid*." According to all Protestant accounts, the growth or development of the Christian Church resembled, at the best, that of a miserable tapeworm; whereas, according to the teaching of the Gospels, it was to be like that of a TREE,—a tree "*shooting out great branches*" (*Mark* iv. 32), and giving shelter and protection to "*all nations*" of the world.

Of the schismatical GREEK Church little need here be said,—1*st*, because in all the Articles of Faith controverted by Protestants (with the exception of that of the Pope's Supremacy—distinctly acknowledged by the Greek Church itself in the great Councils of EPHESUS and CHALCEDON; see Father Gallwey's *Lectures on Ritualism*, Nos. 7 and 8), that Church has always been at one with the Catholic Church; and, 2*dly*, because the Eastern Church, since its separation from the rest of Christendom, has never been· in any sense a *Missionary* Church; and could make no pretensions to the possession of those essential marks of the true Church above referred to,—viz., *Catholicity, Unity*, &c. (see DE MAISTRE on *The Pope*, Eng. trans., pp. 308-340).

Dr. MILMAN (late Dean of St. Paul's) says :—" At the extinction of Paganism, Greek, or, as it may now be called, in opposition to the West, Eastern Christianity, had almost ceased to be aggressive or creative. Except the contested conversion of the Bulgarians, later of the Russians, and a few wild tribes, it *achieved no conquests*. . . . The Greek hierarchy had now [a few centuries later] lost their unity of action, . . . the Bishop of Constantinople was the passive victim, the humble slave, or the factious adversary of the Byzantine Emperor. . . . The lower clergy sank downward into the common ignorance, and yielded to that worst barbarism—a worn-out civilisation " (*Hist. of Latin Christianity*, Introduct., vol. i. ed. 1867) " *The effete and hopeless East* " (*Ib.* vol. ii. p. 413).

NEANDER, the German (Protestant) Church historian, says that "in the Greek Church . . . all true intellectual progress had long since been suppressed by a political and spiritual despotism " (*Hist. of the Church*, Bohn's edit., vol. v. p. 233); and that " the healthful and free evolution of the Church and of theology among the Greeks was hindered by two causes—the despotism of the civil government, before which everything crouched — the Bishops themselves not seldom consenting to act as its humble instruments; and the extinction of the sense of truth, the spirit of insincerity, already a predominant trait which had stamped itself on the entire life of the people " (*Ib.* vol. vi. p. 261). And again : —" In comparison with the fulness of life, manifesting itself under such a variety

fulfilled (in fact, it is notorious that NO SINGLE NATION OF THE EARTH WAS EVER YET CONVERTED FROM HEATHENISM BY PROTESTANT AGENCY OR TO THE PROFESSION OF PROTESTANT CHRISTIANITY); nor can it be pretended that, before the sixteenth century, there existed throughout the world any body of PROTESTANT "*Pastors and Teachers*," which had been provided by God "*for the perfecting of the Saints, for the work of the Ministry, for the edifying of the Body of Christ;*" and for bringing all men to "*meet in the unity of the faith*," and so preserving them therein, that they were no longer liable to be "*tossed to and fro, and carried about by the blasts of false and heretical doctrine*" (*Ephes.* iv. 11-15). In fact, no Protestant can for a moment admit that "the nations" *were*, during many centuries preceding the pretended Reformation, "*taught to observe all things whatsoever Christ had commanded*," or that that Church, which did, in point of fact, "*teach*" them, was "THE PILLAR AND FOUNDATION OF THE TRUTH," and "GUIDED INTO ALL TRUTH BY THE SPIRIT OF TRUTH," when she did so.[1]

of forms, and moving in such various directions, in the Church of the West, the *Greek* Church presents a melancholy spectacle of stiff and torpid uniformity. While the ecclesiastical monarchy of the West could lead onward the mental development of the nations to the age of majority, could permit and promote freedom and variety within certain limits—the brute force of Byzantine despotism, on the other hand, stifled and checked every free movement" (*Ib.* vol. viii. p. 244).

MARSDEN says :—"Buried beneath the ruins of a fallen empire, the Eastern Church drags on a lingering existence. . . . *In tracing the expiring form of this decayed fabric, we search in vain for those striking features which mark her ambitious rival of the West*" (*Dict. of Christian Churches and Sects*, London, 1855).

HALLAM declares his conviction that "the Greek Church, notwithstanding the leniency with which Protestant writers have treated it, *was always more corrupt and intolerant than the Latin*" (*Middle Ages*, ch. ix. part ii. *note*). Compare Dr. ISAAC TAYLOR's *Ancient Christianity*, vol. ii. pp. 173, 192, 205, 213, 214, &c. ; and Professor J. H. TODD's *Discourses on the Prophecies relating to Antichrist*, pp. 330, 342, 351.

[1] The HOMILY OF THE CHURCH OF ENGLAND, *On Peril of Idolatry*, part iii., declares that "clergy and laity, learned and unlearned, ALL AGES, SECTS, AND DEGREES OF MEN, WOMEN, AND CHILDREN, OF WHOLE CHRISTENDOM, HAVE BEEN AT ONCE DROWNED IN DAMNABLE IDOLATRY, AND THAT BY THE SPACE OF EIGHT HUNDRED YEARS AND MORE."

CHILLINGWORTH says that "ALL THE VISIBLE CHURCHES IN THE WORLD had degenerated from the purity of the Gospel," and that the Church was

Even during the few centuries of the existence of Protestantism, notwithstanding the immense advantages and facilities which the invention of *printing*, and a remarkable combination of favourable circumstances—literary, commercial, and political—have placed in the hands of its missionaries (enabling them to scatter abroad, as they themselves boast, *hundreds of millions* of copies of Bibles, New Testaments, and other books, translated into the languages of all known countries of the world), it is certain that the most signal failure has attended all their efforts to convert heathen nations;[1]

"CORRUPTED UNIVERSALLY" (*Religion of Protestants*, chap. v. sects. 13 and 27).

Dr. PERKINS:—"We say that before the days of Luther, FOR THE SPACE OF MANY HUNDRED YEARS, AN UNIVERSAL APOSTASY OVERSPREAD THE WHOLE FACE OF THE EARTH, AND THAT OUR CHURCH WAS NOT THEN VISIBLE TO THE WORLD" (*On the Creed*, p. 400).

Dr. ISAAC TAYLOR not only admits, but proves at length, the "UNIVERSALITY" of the distinctive doctrines and practices of the "Romish" and Greek Churches even in the fourth century. "Scarcely a writer, if there be one," he says, "of the NICENE Church—Eastern or Western—would withhold his contributions to the mass [of evidence producible]: and alas! what a volume would Augustine alone furnish!" (*Ancient Christianity*, vol. ii. p. 213).

[1] This is proved very fully and elaborately in MARSHALL'S great work—*Christian Missions, their Agents, their Method, and their Results* (2 vols., 2d edit., Longmans & Co.)—in which hundreds of testimonies are collected from *Protestant* authors, "of all classes and creeds—English and American, German and French, Swedish and Dutch; historians and naturalists, civil and military officials, tourists and merchants, chaplains and missionaries"—a host of careful and accurate observers, who, as Mr. M. remarks, may be regarded as "witnesses employed by Divine Providence, without their knowledge or concurrence, to detect and expose to the world a fact which the eager passions and prejudices of men would otherwise combine to conceal." By the acknowledgments made by them stand clearly revealed, on the one hand, the utter and universal failure of *Protestant* missions in all parts of the world, notwithstanding the incredibly large sums that, during the present century, have been annually expended upon them; and, on the other, the marvellous results which, during the last three centuries and a half, as in all former ages, have everywhere attended the labours of the *Catholic* missionaries, and this generally under circumstances the most discouraging and disadvantageous from a worldly point of view.

Reviewing this work of Marshall's, the NORTH BRITISH REVIEW, edited by Dr. HANNA, a well-known Presbyterian divine, said:—

"During the sixteenth and seventeenth centuries, *the Romish Church girded the globe with her missions*, planting the Cross from beyond the Wall of China to the Peruvian Cordilleras. Nor is it to be denied that her missionaries in those years were men abounding in Christian heroism and sacrifices. *Of monetary means at her disposal, she had not so much as any one of our Protestant societies.* But she

and so far from the professors of Protestantism presenting, either at home amongst themselves, or to the heathen to whom they send missionaries abroad, a spectacle of RELIGIOUS UNITY—" ONE FOLD," " ONE BODY," " ONE FAITH,"

had, what, alas ! we so often fail to get, abundance of large-hearted men, ready to do and suffer everything for the faith." And again :—" This interesting inquiry," as to the wonderful success of the Catholic, as contrasted with the signal failure of the Protestant missions, " is one the solution of which calls for deeper thought and greater fairness than polemical divines have yet allowed it ; for the student of history will not be satisfied without some theory or law adequate to account for THE UNDENIABLE FACT THAT HITHERTO THE PROGRESS OF CHRISTIANITY AMONGST THE HEATHEN HAS CHIEFLY BEEN CARRIED ON BY ROMANISM, AND ONLY IN A SLIGHT MANNER AS YET BY A CONSISTENT AND SCRIPTURAL PROTESTANTISM " (*North British Review*, May 1864, p. 433).

With Archdeacon PALEY's reflections on the " *little progress* " and " *inconsiderable effect* " of PROTESTANT missions, up to the time when he wrote his *Evidences of Christianity* (see part ii. ch. ix. sect. 3), it is instructive to contrast the account given by another Protestant, the German historian RANKE, of the wonderful success of the CATHOLIC missions about the end of the sixteenth and beginning of the seventeenth centuries :—

" In the beginning of the seventeenth century," he says, " we find the proud fabric of the Catholic Church completely erected in SOUTH AMERICA. It possessed five archbishoprics, twenty-seven bishoprics, four hundred monasteries, with parish churches and ' doctrinas ' innumerable. . Magnificent cathedrals had been reared, the most gorgeous of all, perhaps, being that of Los Angeles. The Jesuits taught grammar and the liberal arts ; they had also a theological seminary attached to their college of San Ildefonso in Mexico. In the universities of Mexico and Lima all the branches of theology were studied. . . . Christianity was, meanwhile, in course of gradual and regular diffusion throughout South America, the mendicant Orders being more particularly active. The conquests had become changed into a seat of missions, and the missions were rapidly proclaiming civilisation." . . .

" A similar process was at the same time in action through EAST INDIA, so far as the rule of the Portuguese extended. Catholicism obtained a central position of great value in Goa. Thousands were converted every year ; even as early as 1565, 300,000 of these newly-made Christians were computed to be in and around Goa, in the mountains of Cochin, and at Cape Comorin. . . . In the year 1609, Father Nobili had already converted seventy *Brahmins*." . . .

" The labours undertaken at the same time in the court of the EMPEROR AKBAR were no less remarkable. . . . In the year 1599, Christmas was celebrated at Lahore with the utmost solemnity. . . . The Christians made great progress. After the death of Akbar, three princes of the blood-royal were solemnly baptized. . . . Christianity seemed gradually to acquire a position of fixed character, although with certain vicissitudes. . . . In 1621 a college was founded in Agra and a station was established at Patna. In 1624 there were hopes that the Emperor Jehanguire would himself become a convert." . . .

" The Jesuits had made their way in CHINA at the same period. . . . In 1611 the first church in Nankin was consecrated, and in 1616 Christian churches are

&c.—it is but too notorious that their profound religious discords and dissensions—all arising from that first and fundamental *principle* of their religion, " THE LIBERTY OF PRIVATE JUDGMENT," and resulting in the formation of innumerable Sects,[1] hopelessly divided against one another in Faith and Communion—have been, almost from the first year of its existence, and in every country where Protestantism has

described as existing in five different provinces of the empire. . . . There passed no year that they did not convert thousands, while those who opposed them gradually became extinct." . . .

" In the year 1577, 300,000 Christians were computed to have received baptism in JAPAN. Father Velignano, who died in 1606, . . . was himself the founder of three hundred churches, and thirty houses for Jesuits in Japan. . . . After the year 1612, they were subjected to fearful persecutions. But they maintained their ground with great steadiness. Their proselytes invoked the death of the martyr, and they had established a fraternity of martyrs, the members of which mutually encouraged each other to the endurance of every possible infliction : they distinguished those years as the *Æra Martyrum*. But despite the increasing violence of the persecutions, their historians affirm that even at that dangerous period new converts were continually added to their numbers. They give the exact amount of 239,339 as that of the converts to Christianity among the Japanese from 1603 to 1622." . . .

" In all these countries . . . the Jesuits *made progress beyond all that they could have hoped for,* and succeeded in conquering, at least partially, the resistance of the national forms of religion that were paramount in the East " (RANKE's *Hist. of the Popes,* Bohn's edit., vol. ii. pp. 228–235).

Lord MACAULAY thus contrasts the Catholic and Protestant Churches during the sixteenth and seventeenth centuries :—

" As the Catholics *in zeal and union* had a great advantage over the Protestants, so had they also *an infinitely superior organisation.* In truth, PROTESTANTISM FOR AGGRESSIVE PURPOSES HAD NO ORGANISATION AT ALL. The Reformed Churches were mere national Churches. The Church of England existed for England alone. It was an institution as purely local as the Court of Common Pleas, and was utterly without any machinery for foreign operations. The Church of Scotland in like manner existed for Scotland alone. THE OPERATIONS OF THE CATHOLIC CHURCH, ON THE OTHER HAND, TOOK IN THE WHOLE WORLD " (*Essays,* vol. iii. p. 236).

During the present century, as already observed, Protestants have expended annually enormous sums on " Missions to the Heathen ; " but, as regards *results,* the CHRISTIAN REMEMBRANCER declared in 1859, that "*we should not allow a few isolated instances of success here and there to blind us to what we must call, to speak plainly, the failure of missionary efforts in modern times*" (*Christ. Remembr.,* vol. 37, p. 69) ; and similar admissions are made by later Protestant writers. (See MARSHALL's *Christ. Miss.* passim).

[1] STAPHYLUS and Cardinal HOSIUS reckoned 270 Sects of Protestants before the end of the sixteenth century. HALLAM reckons "*the growing dissensions and virulence of the Protestants*" among the causes which powerfully tended to make

shown itself, an opprobrium and disgrace to the very name of Christianity.[1]

V. Hence it inevitably follows, that no Protestant Sect or conglomeration of Sects can constitute or represent that, One, True, and Original Church, founded by Christ for the propagation and extension of His One true Faith and Religion throughout the whole world, and for the preservation of that same Faith and Religion throughout all ages; and to which, *in the performance and execution of* the commission assigned to it, He had guaranteed the most perfect success, and *exemption from all liability to failure or error*, by the promise of His own perpetual and efficacious assistance, and the infallible guidance of the Spirit of Truth :—

"Go, teach all nations ; and lo! I am with you always, even to the end of the world."[2]

the learned Grotius seek refuge in the Catholic Communion (*Hist. of Literature*, vol. ii. p. 409, ed. 1860). "Lutherans and Calvinists," says Ranke, "stood opposed to each other with a feeling of mutual hatred ; . . . Episcopalians and Puritans, Arminians and Gomarists, attacked each other with the fiercest hate" (*Hist. of the Popes*, B. vii. ch. ii. sect. 1).

[1] See Balmez's *European Civilisation—Catholicism and Protestantism Compared ;*—especially chap. xlv. :—" *The universal progress of Christianity impeded by Protestantism ;*" also Marshall's *Christian Missions*, passim.

[2] "Always, to the end of the world,"—ἕως τῆς συντελείας τοῦ αἰῶνος. This phrase occurs elsewhere in the Gospels (*Matt.* xiii. 39, 40, 49, xxiv. 3, &c.), and, as Bloomfield says, is "always employed in this sense, of THE WORLD'S END."

With regard to the pronoun "*you*" ("lo! I am with you," &c.), it is hardly necessary to observe, that the use of it no more limits either the Commission or the Promise to the Apostles *personally*, than did the use of the pronoun "*we*" in 1 *Cor.* xv. 51, 1 *Thess.* iv. 17, imply that St. Paul, and those to whom he was writing, would themselves be living on the earth until the Day of Judgment. Christ addressed the Apostles as a BODY CORPORATE ; and, according to the common saying, "a Body Corporate *never dies*." The "LIGHT OF THE WORLD" was not to be diminished through the death or defection of particular members of the Teaching Body ; and it should be observed, that the promise given to this latter, of Christ's perpetual presence and assistance *in the execution of* the Commission assigned to it, was given to it—*not* for *its own* sake or benefit, but—for the good of those ("*all nations*") whom it was to "disciple," and as a perpetual provision and security for *their* being unerringly instructed in "*all things whatsoever He had commanded.*"

It is. evident, therefore, that in sending "the eleven Apostles" to execute His commission, Christ sent *the whole Body of Pastors, who should derive their mission from Himself, through the Apostles and their legitimate Successors, to the end of time.* His words, therefore, may be thus paraphrased : In commanding you (My Apostles), I command the whole Body of Pastors succeeding you, to "*teach all*

"THE SPIRIT OF TRUTH SHALL ABIDE WITH YOU FOR
EVER: HE SHALL GUIDE YOU INTO ALL TRUTH."

"Not for these only do I pray, but for them also who shall
believe on Me through their word: THAT THEY ALL MAY
BE ONE, IN ORDER THAT THE WORLD MAY BELIEVE THAT
THOU HAST SENT ME."

VI. On the other hand, it follows no less certainly, that
that Church which alone *has* had a Visible Existence in all

nations." In commanding you, I command them, to *"baptize all nations."* In
promising to be with you, I promise to be *with them* in the execution of My commission, and in the work of the ministry. *"And behold I am with you always,
even to the end of the world."*

CHRIST intended His CHURCH to be propagated in ALL nations, and to exist in
ALL ages ; and for the securing of this end, "He ordained that there should be *a
race and succession of Apostolic Ministers*, teaching His Doctrines, administering
His Sacraments, and enforcing the observance of His Precepts, in all nations and
ages ; for it was by the introduction of the DOCTRINES of Christ, of the SACRA-
MENTS of Christ, and of the PRECEPTS and INSTITUTIONS of Christ, into all
nations, that THE CHURCH of Christ was to be established in all nations, by the
ministry of those to whom He gave this commission" (*Poynter*).

The promise, *"I am with you always,"* is equivalent to that in *John* xiv. 16,
and xvi. 12 : "The Spirit of Truth *shall abide with you for ever ; He shall guide
you into all truth ;"* and its force becomes more apparent by a comparison with
other passages in Scripture, where, after giving a COMMISSION of peculiar difficulty to man, God adds the promise, *"I will be with you,"* as a guarantee and
security of the possibility and certainty of its fulfilment. See especially *Gen.* xxxi.
3, xlvi. 3, 4 ; *Exod.* iii. 11, 12 ; *Jer.* i. 17, 19. See also *Gen.* xxvi. 3, 24 ; *Deut.*
xxxi. 23 ; *Josh.* i. 5, 9, iii. 7 ; *Judges* vi. 15, 16 ; 2 *Kings* vii. 9 ; *Isai.* xli. 10, xliii.
2, 5 ; *Jer.* xv. 20, xlii. 11 ; *Acts* xviii. 9, 10 ; &c. (Compare *Gen.* xxi. 22, xxviii.
20, xxxix. 2, 3, 21, 23 ; *Deut.* ii. 7, xxxi. 8 ; *Josh.* xiv. 12 ; 1 *Kings* iii. 19, x. 7 ;
2 *Kings* v. 10 ; 1 *Chron.* xxviii. 20 ; *Ps.* xxiii. 4, 5 ; *Jer.* xx. 11 ; *Luke* i. 28, 66 ;
John iii. 2, viii. 29 ; *Acts* x. 38, xi. 21 ; &c.) From these passages it appears that
when a promise or assurance is given that God *"would be with"* any person, it is
always signified that God *so protected and aided that person by His special providence, that whatsoever he undertook should infallibly succeed ;* but this conclusion is
of course most obvious when—as in the first passages referred to—the promise is
given with special reference to the *difficulty* of some undertaking, or in connection
with a *Commission* (such as that in *Matt.* xxviii.) *incapable of accomplishment by
any merely human means.*

When, therefore, our Lord promised to *"be with"* the Teaching Body, in the
execution of the Commission assigned to it, *"always to the end of the world,"* that
promise implied, and was a guarantee, 1st, that the Teaching Body *should exist
indefectibly to the end of the world ;* and 2dly, that throughout the whole course of
its existence it *should be divinely guarded and assisted in fulfilling the Commission
given to it*, viz., in instructing the nations in "all things whatsoever Christ has
commanded ;" in other words, that it should be their INFALLIBLE GUIDE AND
TEACHER.

ages from the time of Christ, which *can* "unroll the catalogue of her Bishops" (TERTULLIAN, *De Præscript. Hæret.*,
c. 32), and prove their continuous succession from the Apostles
of Christ; which *has* fulfilled, or been always engaged in
fulfilling, the Commission which He gave to her, by "discipling" and receiving into her communion by Baptism "all
the nations" of the earth;—that Church whose exhibition
of perfect and supernatural Unity *did* lead an unbelieving
"world" to recognise the Divine Mission of her Founder;
and which alone possesses—and alone claims to possess—that
Divinely-established TEACHING AUTHORITY, by means of
which that Unity was and is secured;—it follows, I say, that
that Church must be the alone True and Original One, which
He Himself founded, and to which the Promises were made.

VII. But, as is most clearly demonstrable, it is of THE
ROMAN CATHOLIC CHURCH,[1] and of her ALONE, that all this
can be truly said.

SHE ALONE has "discipled and baptized" all those nations
of the world which have ever yet received the Christian
Faith, including all those which now profess Protestantism,
and which in the sixteenth century apostatised from that
faith to which they had originally been converted from their
heathenism,[2] and that Church by which, and into which, they

---

[1] By the term *Roman Catholic Church* is meant *the Catholic Church in communion with the See of Rome.* St. Peter's first See was that of Antioch, where
"the disciples were first called Christians" (*Acts* xi. 26); but the Primatial Chair
was subsequently transferred by him to the Imperial City, which thus, as St. LEO
the Great remarks, became the Head of the world in a spiritual sense—"ruling
more widely by divine religion than by earthly empire" (*Serm.* 81). From an
early date the Faith of the Roman Church was "renowned in all the world"
(*Rom.* i. 8, xvi. 19, 20); and, as the French sceptic M. RENAN remarks, it was
through the Papacy that the Christian Church really became Catholic:—" *The
Pope of Rome*," he says, "*has made Christianity the religion of the world*"
(*Hibbert Lectures*, 1880, Eng. trans., p. 122).

[2] Dean MILMAN says:—" All these conquests of Christianity were, in a certain
sense, the conquests *of the Roman See.* . . . *Reverence for Rome penetrated with
the Gospel to the remotest parts.* Germany was converted to Latin Christianity.
Rome was the source, the centre, the regulating authority recognised by the
English apostles of the Teutons. *The clergy were constantly visiting Rome as the
religious capital of the world*, . . . *and bishops from the remotest parts of the
Empire, and of regions never penetrated by the Roman arms, looked to Rome as the
parent of their faith—if not to an infallible, at least to the highest authority in*

(26)

had been baptized. SHE ALONE has been in all ages "*the Light of the world,*" "*a City set on a hill, that could not be hid;*" SHE ALONE "the Pillar and Foundation of the Truth," rendering it conspicuous, and the knowledge of it attainable to all mankind; SHE ALONE that Heavenly Kingdom, the

Christendom" (B. iv. ch. vi. vol. ii. p. 307); "*The Metropolis of Christianity*" (*Ib.* ch. v. p. 299).

And again :—"With all the Teutonic part of Latin Christendom, *the belief in the supremacy of the Pope was coeval with their Christianity;* it was an article of their original creed as much as the Redemption ; their apostles were commissioned by the Pope; to him they humbly looked for instruction and encouragement, even almost for permission to advance upon their sacred adventure. Augustine, Boniface, Ebbo, Anschar, had been *papal missionaries*" (B. vii. ch. i. vol. iv. p. 4).

VENERABLE BEDE, speaking of the conversion of our own country by Augustine and his monks, sent by Pope Gregory the Great, says :—"And whereas he [Pope Gregory] *bore the Pontifical power over all the world, and was placed over the Churches already reduced to the faith of truth, he made our nation, till then given up to idols, the Church of Christ*" (*Hist. Eccles.*, lib. ii. c. 1). Compare Dean MILMAN's chapter on the *Conversion of England* (B. iv. ch. iii. vol. ii. p. 224 *seq.*); NEANDER (vol. v. p. 13 *seq.*); and GUIZOT (*Hist. of European Civilisation*, Bohn's Eng. trans., vol. ii. p. 173, 174). MILMAN further remarks, that "a native clergy seems to have grown up more rapidly in Britain than in any other of the Teutonic kingdoms. *But they were in general the admiring pupils of the Roman clergy. To them Rome was the centre and source of the faith,*" &c. (*loc. cit.* p. 249).

RANKE, the German Protestant historian, also says, that "together with the doctrines of Christianity, a veneration for Rome and for the Holy See, such as had never before existed in any nation, found place among the Germanic Britons" (*Hist. of the Popes*, Bohn's edit., vol. i. p. 11).

On St. Boniface, the apostle of Germany, and the conversion of that country to the faith of Rome, see NEANDER (vol. v. pp. 62, 65, 66, 69, 75, 87, 88, 98, &c.), and MILMAN (B. iv. ch. v. vol. ii. p. 295 *seq.*). NEANDER gives Boniface's oath of obedience to the Pope (*loc. cit.* p. 66).

RANKE says :—"Boniface, the apostle of the Germans, was an Anglo-Saxon ; this missionary, largely sharing in the veneration professed by his nation for St. Peter and his successors, *had from the beginning voluntarily pledged himself to abide faithfully by all the regulations of the Roman See: to this promise he most religiously adhered.* On all the German Churches founded by him was imposed an extraordinary obligation to obedience. Every Bishop was required expressly to promise that his whole life should be passed in unlimited obedience to the Romish Church, to St. Peter and his representatives" (*op. cit.* p. 12).

M. GUIZOT says that "for him [Boniface] *Rome is the centre, the Pope is the chief of Christianity*" (*op. cit.* vol. ii. p. 175). He gives his oath of submission to the Pope, and his account of the first German Council, held under his presidency in 742, and adds :—"Of a surety, it is impossible more formally to submit the new Church, the new Christian nations, to the Papal power" (*Ib.* p. 177).

MILMAN, after describing his "wonderful successes," says :—"Boniface *had*

"*mustard-seed*" of the Parable, which, from a very small germ, quickly grew and increased until it "*became a great tree,*" overshadowing the earth, and giving shelter and protection to "the fowls of the air;" SHE ALONE the "*net,*" which, cast into the sea of the world, has "*gathered of every kind;*" SHE ALONE "*the leaven,*"[1] which, "*hid in the three measures of meal*" (the three parts, then known, of the world), has effected a change and spiritual revolution throughout the earth; and will not cease to do so "*until the whole be leavened,*" *i.e.,* until the Faith of Christ and her Spiritual Dominion shall have been propagated and extended throughout every part and corner of the world.[2]

won a new empire to Christianity, and was placed over it as spiritual sovereign by the respectful gratitude of the Pope. He received the pall of a Metropolitan, and was empowered as primate to erect bishoprics throughout Germany. Again he visited Rome, and was invested by Gregory III., the new Pope, with full powers as representative of the Apostolic See" (*loc. cit.* p. 300).

For an account of the conversion to Christianity of Denmark, Sweden, Norway, and other Northern countries (now Protestant), by missionaries sent by the Popes, in the ninth, tenth, and eleventh centuries, the Protestant reader can refer to NEANDER (vol. v. pp. 373–477), or Dean JOSEPH MILNER'S *Church History* (cent. viii. ch. v., cent. ix. ch. v. &c.).

[1] Regarding the prophetic significance of these three parables—of the *mustard-seed,* the *net,* and the *leaven*—see the notes from TRENCH *On the Parables* (*sup.* pp. 6, 7); also GRESWELL *On the Parables* (vol. ii. pp. 175 *seq.,* 259, 261, 265).

Several Protestant writers, despairing of finding any non-Catholic Church to which these parables could be applied, have actually dared to maintain that they were prophetic of the universality of the kingdom of *Antichrist* or of *Satan,* and of the universal *corruption* of Christianity, through the spread of "Popery" and the "dominion of a proud world-hierarchy;" thus exactly fulfilling our Lord's prediction :—"*If they have called the Master of the house Beelzebub, much more them of His household*" (*Matt.* x. 25, and xii. 24–28). Dr. TRENCH speaks of the holders of this opinion as being "little bands of modern Separatists, whose motive of course is obvious" (p. 112); yet he takes the trouble to refute them at some length.

[2] For copious information (chiefly in the form of Protestant testimonies) regarding Catholic Missions in modern times, the reader should consult Mr. MARSHALL'S work above mentioned. The Anglican CHURCH TIMES of January 23, 1880, says :—"Missions to the heathen have always been a strong point in the Roman Church. Her organisation for these enterprises is on so vast and complete a scale compared with any other branch of the Church; the training of her ministers for distant spheres of labour is so directly pointed to the end to be attained; their zeal and self-sacrifice causing them to exhibit the Church before the heathen as a body called to suffer for Christ's sake; their entire freedom from earthly ties; the implicit and unquestioning obedience which is required of them to the powers above them; and last, and not least, the peculiar knack which Rome has with

This CATHOLIC CHURCH—of which the See of Peter was ever the acknowledged Centre and Head [1]—ALONE was [2] (as

few exceptions exercised, of putting the right man in the right place, have all conduced to attract and win the sympathies of heathen hearts. And while we acknowledge and admire the earnest zeal, and self-devotion, and perseverance which have characterised the missionaries themselves, we may recognise also a spirit of discretion in much of the instrumentality that is provided ; the numerous bodies sent out together, the establishment of sanctuaries and religious houses for the reception of catechumens and the education of orphans and native children, the preparation of elementary forms of instruction, such as those of Francis Xavier, for the use of the catechists in India, the community of living and austerity of habits invariably adopted, have doubtless contributed to the success which, however much exaggerated in many cases, and however ephemeral in others, has on the whole attended the missionary efforts of the Roman Communion in all parts of the globe."

[1] See CATHEDRA PETRI, 2d ed., Burns & Oates.

[2] "The phrase 'Catholic Church,'" says M. RENAN, "speaking of the second century, "breaks upon us from all sides at once, as the name of THE GREAT COMMUNION WHICH IS DESTINED THENCEFORTH TO COME DOWN THE AGES IN UNBROKEN UNITY" (Hibbert Lectures, 1880, Eng. trans., p. 164).

"The Clergy," says Dean MILMAN, "including the Monks and Friars, were ONE throughout Latin Christendom; and through them, to a great extent, the Latin Church was ONE. . . . The Pope's awful powers held in check the constant inevitable tendency to rebellion and contumacy, which was usually that of individual Prelates or small factions. . . . On the whole, the Order of the Clergy was ONE FROM THE UTMOST EAST TO THE FARTHER WEST, FROM THE NORTH TO THE SOUTH" (Hist. of Lat. Christ., B. xiv. ch. i. vol. ix. pp. 25, 27). And again :—" Latin Christendom, or rather universal Christendom, was ONE (excepting those who were self-outlawed, or outlawed by the dominant authority from the Christian Monarchy), not only in the organisation of the all-ruling Hierarchy, and the admission of Monkhood ; it was ONE IN THE GREAT SYSTEM OF BELIEF. . . . The whole world was ONE IN THE POPULAR RELIGION " (Ib. ch. ii. pp. 53, 54). M. GUIZOT, also, remarks that this great fact of "the UNITY of the Church, the UNITY of the Christian' society, despite all the diversities of time, place, domination, language, or origin," is one "which dominates over all, which characterises the Christian Church in general, and has, as it were, decided her destiny." " This," he adds, "is a great and glorious fact, and one which, from the fifth to the thirteenth century, has rendered immense services to humanity. The mere fact of the unity of the Church maintained some tie between countries and nations that everything else tended to separate ; under its influence, some general notions, some sentiments of a vast sympathy continued to be developed ; and from the very heart of the most frightful political confusion that the world has ever known arose, perhaps, the most extensive and the purest idea that has ever rallied mankind—the idea of spiritual society; for that is the philosophical name of the Church, the type which she wished to realise " (Hist. of European Civilisation, Bohn's Eng. trans., vol. ii. pp. 19, 20).

Protestants often ask triumphantly—" Where was the Unity of the Catholic Church at the time of the great PAPAL SCHISM (A.D. 1378-1417), during which the nations of Europe were divided in their allegiance to three contending Popes ? "

she still is [1]), the "*One Fold under One Shepherd,*"—that great and illustrious Body or Society of Christians, whose exhibition of supernatural and majestic Unity struck "*the World*" with awe and amazement, causing it to recognise the Divine Mission of her Founder and Head,—so that "*the kingdoms*

—To which objection it may be replied :—*1st,* That the Church's Unity of *Faith, Public Worship,* and *Sacraments,* remained intact during that whole period ; *2dly,* that what may be called the *interregnum* in the Church, caused by the controversy regarding the validity of the election of the claimants to the Papacy, was abnormal in its character and transient in its effects; and that the Church all along retained—and ultimately exercised—the power of determining who was or should be her validly elected Head. It was not promised to the Church that she should not be assaulted by the gates of hell (the Powers of Darkness), but that she should always prove victorious against them.

[1] Lord MACAULAY, in a well-known passage, says :—" The Papacy remains, not in decay, not a mere antique, but full of life and youthful vigour. The Catholic Church is still sending forth to the farthest ends of the world missionaries as zealous as those who landed in Kent with Augustine, and still confronting hostile kings with the same spirit with which she confronted Attila. The number of her children is greater than in any former age. . . . She saw the commencement of all the Governments and of all the ecclesiastical institutions that are now in the world ; and we feel no assurance that she is not destined to see the end of them all. She was great and respected before the Saxon had set foot on Britain, before the Frank had crossed the Rhine, when Grecian eloquence still flourished in Antioch, when idols were still worshipped in the temple of Mecca. And she may still exist in undiminished vigour when some traveller from New Zealand shall, in the midst of a vast solitude, take his stand on a broken arch of London Bridge, to sketch the ruins of St. Paul's " (*Essay on Ranke's Lives of the Popes*).

As farther illustrating and corroborating what has been said above, regarding that spectacle of UNIVERSALITY and of MAJESTIC UNITY which the Catholic Church presents to the world at large, the following extracts from the leading articles and special correspondence of the chief English journals, at the time of the opening of the Œcumenical Council of the Vatican, may perhaps be of interest to the reader :—

STANDARD (December 10th, 1869) :—" In historic importance, in traditional dignity, in the splendour of the associations that gather round its name, no Assembly in the world, past or present, can pretend to compare with the great Parliament of the Latin Church. The unbroken continuity of the history of that Church, its undeniable and uninterrupted descent from the Church founded by the Apostles, renders this Council . . . the immediate successor and representative, in a sense in which no other Council can rival its claims, of the Council of Nicæa, if not of the Council of Jerusalem. Nor is its actual power and consequence unworthy of its traditional heritage. . . . It is the representative assembly, the omnipotent legislature of a compact and coherent body of Christians, whose number approaches more nearly to two than one hundred millions," &c.

After referring to the attempts made by the enemies of the Pope and of the Church to hinder the assembling of the Council, the special correspondent (STANDARD, Dec. 11th) says :—" Nevertheless, all has been in vain ; and the dispassionate observer is compelled to confess that the spectacle of so many

of this world became the Kingdom of our Lord and of His Christ" (Rev. xi. 15). SHE ALONE possesses—and alone claims to possess—that supreme and unerring Teaching Authority, without which no such Unity could be guaranteed or preserved.[1] In—and by—HER ALONE have all those

hundreds of Bishops, coming from the farthest quarters of the earth at the beck of an old man, powerless in all but spiritual thunderbolts, is one that, occurring in the nineteenth century, and especially at this period of it, is calculated to strike the believing with a pious admiration, and even the incredulous, like ourselves, with irrepressible astonishment."

The DAILY NEWS (Dec. 14th) :—"It must be admitted that, weak as is the temporal power of the Pope, no other Prince could have assembled such a body as met to-day in the Council-hall of St. Peter's, and no other could have provided them with such a magnificent temple. From the remotest quarters of the globe —from a land that was but just heard of when the Council of Trent sat, from a land that was then wholly unknown,—from Palestine and Syria, the cradles of Christianity ; from Persia, from China, from India, from Africa, from the Western Isles, as well as from the countries washed by the Mediterranean, men of various tongues and of diverse origin, men of great learning and of great age, have come together to this famous city, in obedience—voluntary and spiritual obedience— to the Pastor who claims to be the Successor of Peter, and the Vicegerent of God upon earth."

The TIMES (Dec. 16th) :—"Seven hundred Bishops, more or less, representing all Christendom, were seen gathered round one altar and one throne, partaking of the same Divine Mystery, and rendering homage, by turns, to the same spiritual authority and power. As they put on their mitres or took them off, and as they came to the steps of the altar or the foot of the common Spiritual Father, it was IMPOSSIBLE NOT TO FEEL THE UNITY AND THE POWER OF THE CHURCH WHICH THEY REPRESENTED."

[1] "In the Catholic Church," says a writer in the UNION REVIEW (May 1875), "it was always an article of faith that our Lord, by the assistance and guidance of His Holy Spirit, preserved the whole Church, in her collective capacity, from falling into error in her dogmatic teaching. But it was also a point of belief, which may be traced up to the Apostolic age, that in the administration of this teaching authority, the See of St. Peter held a supreme office ; that it was the centre of ecclesiastical operations, if we may use such a term ; that apart from it there would be no genuine orthodoxy, no true Catholicity; and that in all the great controversies which from time to time divided the Christian world, the most crucial test of truth was the adherence to any dogma by the See of Peter."

"Though a few distinguished voices have been lifted up against the dogma of Papal Infallibility, they have indeed been, and continue to be, few and far between. We believe there is but one Bishop out of the whole Romish Hierarchy who is not now inculcating the dogma, and that solitary one does not go beyond a passive resistance. . . . Rome, under the guidance of Pius IX., at least knows its own mind, which is more than can be said of perhaps any other influential branch of the Christian Church at the present moment. . . . Were Pius IX. to die to-morrow, he would leave the Roman Church far more powerful than he found it, and endowed with a far higher vitality" (STANDARD, June 19th, 1872).

Prophecies been fulfilled that were uttered regarding the CHURCH OF CHRIST—the KINGDOM OF THE MESSIAS; *e.g.,* that "*Kings should be her nursing fathers, and queens her nursing mothers; they should bow down before her with their face toward the earth, and lick up the dust of her feet;*"—that "*the Gentiles should come to her light, and kings to the brightness of her rising; . . . her gates should be open continually; they should not be shut day nor night; that men might bring unto her the forces of the Gentiles, and that their kings might be brought: for the nation and kingdom that would not serve her should perish;*"—that "*no weapon formed against her should prosper, and every tongue that should arise in judgment against her she should condemn;*"—that God's "*Spirit that should be upon her, and His words which He would put in her mouth, should not depart out of her mouth, nor out of the mouth of her seed, nor out of the mouth of her seed's seed, from henceforth and for ever;*"—that "*from the rising of the sun, even to the going down of the same, God's name should be great among the Gentiles, and in every place incense should be offered to His name, and a pure offering;*"—that *the Messias should be "for a light to the Gentiles, and for salvation unto the ends of the earth;*"—He "*should have the Gentiles for His inheritance, and the uttermost parts of the earth for His possession; He should rule from sea to sea, and from the river unto the ends of the earth, all nations falling down before Him, all nations serving Him;*"—and, finally, that, *in this Church of the Messias,* "*the Lord God would set up a Kingdom which should never be destroyed,*" and "*against which the Gates of Hell should never prevail.*"

We conclude, therefore, that the ROMAN CATHOLIC CHURCH—and she ALONE—is the One true Catholic and Apostolic Church of Christ,—the Church which He Himself founded, and with which, in the performance of her great office as Teacher of the nations, He Himself—"*the Way, the Truth, and the Life*"—promised to abide "*always, even to the end of the world;*" and, consequently, that it is from HER voice and teaching alone that we can with certainty and security learn the entire Faith and body of Doctrines which He has revealed,—"*all things whatsoever He has commanded her to teach to all nations.*"

[1] "The universal aptness of a religious system for all stages of civilisation, and for all sorts and conditions of men, well befits its claim of divine origin. She is of all nations and of all times, that wonderful Church of Rome."—KINGLAKE'S *Eothen*, chap. xi.

"Protestantism was the work of man ; and it appears in no other light even in the history which its own disciples have drawn of its origin."—SCHLEGEL'S *Philosophy of History*, Bohn's 7th Eng. edit., p. 411.

"Notwithstanding all his attempts to deface the work of God, man cannot blot out the eternal characters which distinguish truth from error."—BALMEZ, *European Civilisation, Protestantism and Catholicity Compared*, Eng. trans., p. 45.

APPENDIX.

———•———

Some Testimonies of Protestant and non-Christian Historians regarding the beneficial Action and Influence of the Catholic Church during the Early and Middle Ages, the early and providential Development of the Papal Power, &c., &c.

M. ERNEST RENAN, the well-known French savant and sceptic, in the *Hibbert Lectures*, delivered in London in 1880, speaks as follows :—

"The origins of Christianity form the most heroic episode of the history of humanity. . . . This extraordinary movement, with which no other can be compared, came out of the heart of Judaism. But it is doubtful whether Judaism alone would have conquered the world. For this it was . . . above all needful that the new movement should transfer itself to the Greek and Latin world, and there awaiting the barbarians, should become as it were a leaven in the midst of those European races by means of which humanity accomplishes its destiny."[1] . . . (pp. 8, 9).

"In order that Judea might make a religious conquest of the world, it was necessary that she should be blotted out from the roll of nations. . . . The victory of Rome was complete. . . . The national existence of the Jewish people was irretrievably lost ; but this was a piece of good fortune. The true glory of Judaism was the Christianity then in act of birth. And for Christianity, the destruction of Jerusalem and the Temple was an advantage above all other. . . . The Romans thought that in tearing away the root they were at the same time tearing away the sucker ; but the sucker had already become a tree, with an independent life of its own" (pp. 104, 115, 116).

After showing that "in proportion as the Church of Jerusalem falls the Church of Rome rises," and that "while the Pope of Jerusalem would have smothered Christianity at the end of a century or two, *the Pope of Rome has made it the religion of the world*" (p. 122), he says :—

"The truth of what I have said is illustrated in a very important personage, who appears to have been at the head of the Roman Church

---

[1] M. RENAN'S remarks furnish a remarkable commentary on the words of St. PAUL :—"*If the fall of them* [the Jews] *be the riches of the world, and the diminution of them the riches of the Gentiles ; . . . if the casting away of them be the reconciling of the world,*" &c. (*Rom.* xi. 12, 15, 20).

C

in the last years of the first century. . . . I mean Clement of Rome. . . . The high rank which he held in the purely spiritual hierarchy of the Church of his times, and the unequalled credit which he enjoyed, are beyond doubt. His approval was a law in itself (*Pseudo-Hermas*, vis. ii. 4). All parties claimed his leadership, and desired to shelter themselves beneath his authority. . . . He is the first type of Pope which Church history presents to us. His lofty personality, which legend makes more lofty still, was, after that of Peter, the holiest figure of primitive Christian Rome. Succeeding ages looked upon his venerable face as that of a mild and grave legislator, a perpetual homily of submission and respect.

" Already the idea of a certain primacy belonging to his Church was beginning to make its way to the light. The right of warning other Churches and of composing their differences was conceded to it. Similar privileges—so at least it was believed—had been accorded to Peter by the other disciples (*Luke* xxii. 32). Thus a bond which gradually grew closer was established between Peter and Rome. Grave dissensions tore in pieces the Church of Corinth (Hegesip. in Euseb. *Hist. Eccles.* iii. 16, iv. 22). The Roman Church, consulted as to these troubles, replied in a letter which is still extant. It is anonymous, but a very ancient tradition assigns the composition of it to Clement " (pp. 124, 125).

" The Roman Church was henceforth the Church of order, of rule, of subordination. Its fundamental principle was that humility and submission were of more account than the sublimest gifts. Its letter to the Corinthians is the first manifesto of the principle of authority made within the Christian Church " (p. 127).

" In the primitive Christian community, the importance of Churches was in proportion to their apostolic nobility. The guarantee of orthodoxy was the *diadoche*, the Episcopal succession by which the great Churches were connected with the Apostles. A direct succession was a very strong warrant of agreement in doctrine ; the greatest possible importance was attached to it. But what shall we say of a Church founded both by Peter and Paul ? It is clear that such a Church would be regarded as having a real superiority over all others. To have succeeded in establishing this belief was the masterpiece of that cleverness which characterised the Church of Rome. By the time of Antoninus Pius [A.D. 138] almost everybody had come to believe that Peter and Paul had in perfect agreement founded Christianity at Rome, and had sealed the work with their blood. The ecclesiastical destiny of Rome was thenceforth fixed. When her part in the profane world was played out, this extraordinary city was destined to play another and a sacred part, a part like that of Jerusalem " (p. 148).

After mentioning the attempt of Valentinus to establish a Gnostic school in Rome, and his excommunication by Pope Hyginus, he says :—

" *The centre of a future Catholic orthodoxy was plainly here.* Pius, who succeeded Hyginus, showed the same firmness in defending the purity of the faith. Cerdo, Marcion, Valentinus, Marcellinus, are removed from the Church by the sentence of Pius. *In the reign of Antoninus* [A.D. 138 *seq.*], *the germ of the Papacy already exists in a very definite form.* The Church of Rome shows itself increasingly indifferent to those visionary speculations which were the delight of minds full of the intellectual activity of the Greeks, but, at the same time, corrupted by the dreams of the East. The organisation of Christian society was the chief work pursued at Rome. That wonderful city brought to this task the exclusively practical genius and the powerful moral energy which she has applied in so many different ways. Almost careless of speculation, decisively hostile to novelties in doctrine, she presided, as a mistress already practised in the art, over all the changes which took place in the discipline and the hierarchy of the Church."

"What was in process of development in the Christian Church about the year 120 or 130 was the Episcopate. Now the creation of the Episcopate was evidently the work of Rome" . . . (pp. 148-151). After pronouncing this to be a "complete transformation" in the government of the Church,[1] he says:—

"Nevertheless, this transformation was the essential condition of the energy of Christianity. And a concentration of powers became at once necessary when these Churches grew up to be tolerably numerous: the relations between these little pious societies were possible only so long as they had acknowledged representatives entitled to act for them. It is besides indisputable that, without the Episcopate, Churches brought into union for a moment by the recollection of Jesus would soon have been scattered. Divergencies of doctrine, differences in turn of mind, above all, rivalries, unsatisfied self-appreciations, would have produced their characteristic result of disunion and disintegration without end" (p. 158).

"Thanks to the Church of Rome,[2] the religion of Jesus thus acquired a certain solidity and consistency. The great danger of Gnosticism, which threatened to divide Christendom into innumerable sects, was averted. The phrase 'Catholic Church' breaks upon us from all sides at once, as the name of the great communion which is destined thenceforth to come down the ages in unbroken unity. And the character of this Catholicity is already sufficiently visible. The Montanists are regarded as sectaries; the Marcionites are convicted of falsifying apostolical doctrine; the different Gnostic schools are more and more repelled from the bosom of the general Church. There is, then, something which is neither Montanism, nor Marcionism, nor Gnosticism — unsectarian

---

[1] It is hardly necessary, perhaps, to observe, that M. RENAN's expression of erroneous opinions, on this and some other points, does not detract from the general value of his testimony regarding the predominant authority of the Church of Rome at this early period.

[2] Mr. PALMER of Oxford also says:—"We find that the Roman Church was zealous to maintain the true faith from the earliest period, condemning and expelling the Gnostics, Artemonites, &c.; and during the Arian mania it was the bulwark of the Catholic Faith" (*On the Church*, vol. ii. pt. vi. ch. 3).

Christianity, the Christianity of the majority of Bishops, resisting and using all the sects, having, if you will, none but negative characteristics, but by those negative characteristics preserved from pietistic aberrations and dissolvent rationalism" (pp. 164, 165).

After giving a sketch of the formation of Christendom, and remarking that "the Empire was, as it were, the mould in which the new religion took shape: the inner framework, the limits, the hierarchical divisions of the Church were those of the Empire ; " and that "under Marcus Aurelius the Episcopate is completely ripe : the Papacy exists in germ" (p. 169), he continues :—

"ROME was the place in which this great idea of Catholicity was worked out. *More and more every day it became the capital of Christianity, and took the place of Jerusalem as the religious centre of humanity.* Its Church claimed a precedence over all others which was generally recognised (Iren. iii. 3 ; Tertull. *Præscript.* 21, 36 ; Cyprian, *Epist.* 52, 55, 67, 71, 75 ; Firmilian). All the doubtful questions which agitated the Christian conscience came to Rome to ask for arbitration, if not decision. Men argued, certainly not in a very logical way, that as Christ had made Cephas the corner-stone of His Church, the privilege ought to be inherited by his successors. . . . The Bishop of Rome became the Bishop of bishops, he who admonished all others. Rome proclaims her right—a dangerous right—of excommunicating those who do not walk step by step with her. . . . At the end of the second century we can already recognise, by signs which it is impossible to mistake, the spirit which in 1870 will proclaim the infallibility of the Pope. The writing of which the fragment known as the Canon of Muratori formed a part, and which was produced at Rome about the year 180 A.D., shows us Rome already defining the Canon of Scripture, alleging the martyrdom of Peter as the foundation of Catholicity, repudiating Montanism and Gnosticism alike. Irenæus (*Lib.* iii. 3) refutes all heresies by reference to the belief of this Church, 'the greatest, the oldest, the most illustrious, which possesses, in virtue of an unbroken succession, the true tradition of the Apostles Peter and Paul, and to which, because of its Primacy, all the rest of the Church ought to have recourse'" (pp. 172–174).

" This precedence of the Church of Rome only became more marked in the third century. The Bishops of Rome showed a rare ability in avoiding theological questions, while they kept themselves to the front in all matters of organisation and administration. The tradition of the Roman Church passes for the most ancient of all (Origen, in Euseb. *Hist. Eccles.* vi. 14). Cornelius takes the first place in the affair of Novatianism : we see him, in especial, depriving Italian Bishops and nominating their successors (Letter of Cornelius in Euseb. vi. 43). Rome was also the central authority of the African Churches (Tertull. *Præs.* 21 ; Cyprian. *Epist.* 52, 55, 71, 75)" (p. 176).

After speaking of the injury done to the City of Rome by the Emperor Constantine's transference of the seat of government to Constantinople, and by the invasions of barbarians that followed, he says :—

"Rome's first revenge is taken in the gravity and depth of her organising spirit. What men are St. Sylvester, St. Damasus, St. Gregory the Great! With admirable courage Rome labours for the conversion of the barbarians ; she attaches them to herself ; she makes them her clients, her subjects. The masterpiece of her policy was her alliance with the Carolingian House, and the bold stroke by which she revived in that family the Empire which had been dead for 300 years. The Church of Rome then lifts herself up more powerful than ever, and again, for eight centuries more, becomes the centre of all Western politics" (pp. 198, 199) —RENAN'S *Hibbert Lectures on the Influence of the Institutions, Thought, and Culture of Rome on Christianity and the Development of the Catholic Church*, Eng. trans., 1880).

M. GUIZOT, the Protestant historian of France, speaking of the fifth century, when the Roman Empire was in the agonies of dissolution, and the whole of Europe was inundated by hordes of barbarians,[1] says :—

"I do not think that I say more than the truth in affirming that *it was the Christian Church which saved Christianity ;* it was the Church with its institutions, its magistrates, and its power that vigorously resisted both the internal dissolution of the Empire and barbarism ; which conquered the barbarians, and became the bond, the medium, and the principle of civilisation between the Roman and barbarian worlds. . . . In the midst of that deluge of material force which at this period overwhelmed society, there was an immense benefit in the presence of a moral influence, a moral power, a power which derived all its force from convictions, from belief, from moral sentiments. *Had there been no Christian Church, the whole world would have been abandoned to mere material force. The Church alone exercised a moral power"* (GUIZOT'S *Hist. Gén. de la Civilisation en Europe*, 3d ed., Paris, 1840, 2ème Leçon).

"The Church was a regularly organised society, having its principles, its rules, its discipline, and animated with an ardent desire of extending its influence,[2] of conquering its conquerors. Among the Christians of this period, among the Christian clergy, there were men who had thought

---

[1] "Let us reflect for a moment," says M. GOSSELIN, "on the character of the barbarous hordes which, after the close of the fourth century, partitioned among themselves the members of the Roman Empire in the West. Completely ignorant of the arts and sciences and of civilisation, they knew no other occupation but hunting and war; no law but force ; no glory but conquest ; and, far from feeling the inconveniences and disorder of this savage state, they professed a sovereign contempt for a mode of life more refined. The Christian religion, which they all embraced, softened by degrees their ferocious manners; but this inestimable effect of their conversion was slow and insensible; the majority of them long retained their ancient habits—that is, their inconstant, violent, and ungovernable temper ; their passionate taste for hunting and war ; their profound contempt for the arts and sciences ; and especially the spirit of insubordination and independence, which seemed to be the most deeply marked trait in their character" (*The Power of the Popes during the Middle Ages*, Eng. trans., vol. ii. p. 40).

[2] "After the fifth century, *Papacy* took the lead in the conversion of the Pagans" (GUIZOT'S *Hist. of Civilisation in France*, Bohn's Eng. trans., vol. ii. p. 173).

upon all moral and political questions, who had decided opinions and energetic sentiments upon all subjects, and a vivid desire to propagate and give them empire. No society ever made more vigorous efforts to make her influence felt, and to mould to her own form the world around her, than the Christian Church from the fifth to the tenth century. She had, in a manner, assailed barbarism on all points, to civilise by subduing it" (*Ib.* 3ème Leçon, p. 86).

"All the *civil* elements of modern society [municipal government, the feudal system and royalty] were either in their infancy or in decrepitude. The Church alone was young and organised ; she alone had acquired a settled form, and retained all the vigour of her prime ; she alone had both activity and order, energy and a system, that is, the two great means of influence. . . . The Church had, moreover, agitated all the great questions which concern man ; she was solicitous about all the problems of his nature, about all the chances of his destiny. Hence, her influence on modern civilisation has been immense, greater perhaps than has ever been imagined by her most ardent adversaries or her most zealous advocates. Absorbed either in her defence or in aggression, they considered her only in a polemical point of view, and they have failed, I am convinced, in judging her with fairness, and in measuring her in all her dimensions" (*Ib.* 5ème Leçon, p. 132).

The Rev. H. MILMAN, D.D. (late Dean of St. Paul's), says :— " Christianity, in its Latin form, which for centuries was to be its most powerful, enduring, and prolific development, wanted, for her stability and unity of influence, a capital and a centre ; and Rome might seem deserted by her Emperors for the express purpose of allowing the spiritual monarchy to grow up without any dangerous collision against the civil government. The Emperors had long withdrawn from Rome as the royal residence. Of those who bore the title, one ruled in Constantinople, and, more and more absorbed in the cares and calamities of the Eastern sovereignty, became gradually estranged from the affairs of the West. . . . The Western Emperor lingered for a time in inglorious obscurity among the marshes of Ravenna, till at length the faint shadow of monarchy melted away, and a barbarian assumed the power and the appellation of Sovereign of Italy. Still, of the barbarian kings, not one ventured to fix himself in the ancient capital, or to inhabit the mouldering palaces of the older Cæsars. . . .

" It was not solely as a Christian Bishop, and Bishop of that city which was still, according to the prevailing feeling, the capital of the world, but as the successor of St. Peter, of him who was now acknowledged to be the head of the Apostolic body, that the Roman Pontiff commanded the veneration of Rome and of Christendom. . . . At the commencement of the fifth century, the lineal descent of the Pope from St. Peter was an accredited tenet of Christianity. . . .

" Everything tended to confirm, nothing to impede or to weaken, the gradual condensation of the supreme ecclesiastical power in the Supreme

Bishop. The majesty of the notion of one all-powerful ruler, to which the world had been so long familiarised in the Emperors ; the discord and emulation among the other prelates, both of the East and West, and the manifold advantage of a supreme arbiter ; *the unity of the visible Church*, which was becoming—or had indeed become—the dominant idea of Christendom ;—all seemed to demand, or, at least, had a strong tendency to promote and to maintain, *the necessity of one Supreme Head.* . . .

" In the West, throughout Latin Christendom, the Roman See, in antiquity, in dignity, in the more regular succession of its prelates, stood alone and unapproachable. In the great Eastern bishoprics the holy lineage had been already broken and confused by the claims of rival prelates, by the usurpation of Bishops accounted heretical, at the present period Arians or Macedonians or Apollinarians, later Nestorians or Monophysites "[1] (MILMAN'S *Hist. of Latin Christianity*, Book ii. ch. i. vol. i. p. 104 *seq.*, ed. 1867).

Speaking of the fall of Rome under Alaric, A.D. 410, he says :—" That which might have appeared the most fatal blow to Roman greatness, as dissolving the spell of Roman empire, the capture, the conflagration, the plunder, the depopulation of Rome by the barbarian Goths, tended directly to establish and strengthen the spiritual supremacy of Rome. It was pagan Rome, the Babylon of sensuality, pride, and idolatry, which fell before the triumphant Alaric ; the Goths were the instruments of Divine vengeance against paganism, which lingered in this its last stronghold. Christianity hastened to disclaim all interest, all sympathy, in the fate of ' the harlot that sat on the seven hills ' " (*Ib.* p. 120).

" However the first appalling intelligence of this event shook the Roman world to its centre, and the fearful scene of pillage, violation, and destruction by fire and sword was imagined to surpass in its horrors everything recorded in profane or sacred history, yet the shock passed away, and Rome quietly assumed her second, her Christian empire. . . . Innocent [the Pope] returned to a city, if in some parts ruined and desolate, now entirely Christian : the ancient religion was buried under the ruins. . . . Babylon has fallen, and fallen for ever ; the City of God, at least the centre and stronghold of the City of God, is in Christian Rome" (*Ib.* pp. 130, 136, 138).

" The Pontificate of Leo the Great [A.D. 440] is one of the epochs in the history of Latin, or rather of universal Christianity. Christendom, wherever mindful of its Divine origin and of its proper humanising and hallowing influence, might turn away in shame from these melancholy and disgraceful [religious] contests in the East. *On the throne of Rome alone,*

---

[1] " In the East, religion ceased more and more to be an affair of pure religion. It was mingled up with all the intrigues of the Imperial Court, with all the furies of faction in the great cities. . . . The rivalry of the Sees darkened into the fiercest personal hostility. . . . The deeper the East was sunk in anarchy and confusion, the more commanding the stately superiority of Rome " (*Ib.* ch. iii. pp. 177-195).

of all the greater Sees, did religion maintain its majesty, its sanctity, its piety; and, if it demanded undue deference ; the world would not be inclined rigidly to question pretensions supported as well by such conscious power as by such singular and unimpeachable virtue ; and by such inestimable benefits conferred on Rome, on the Empire, on civilisation. . . .*Supremacy, held by so firm and vigorous a hand as that of Leo, might seem almost necessary to Christendom"* (*Ib.* ch. iv. pp. 228, 254).

Speaking of the close of the sixth century of Christianity, when "anarchy threatened the whole West of Europe, and had already almost enveloped Italy in ruin and destruction," Milman says :—" Now was the crisis in which THE PAPACY must reawaken its obscured and suspended life. *It was the only power which lay not entirely and absolutely prostrate before the disasters of the times—a power which had an inherent strength, and might resume its majesty. It was this power which was most imperatively required to preserve all which was to survive out of the crumbling wreck of Roman civilisation. To Western Christianity was absolutely necessary a centre, standing alone, strong in traditionary reverence and in acknowledged claims to supremacy.* Even the perfect organisation of the Christian hierarchy might in all human probability have fallen to pieces in perpetual conflict ; it might have degenerated into a half-secular feudal caste, with hereditary benefices, more and more entirely subservient to the civil authority, a priesthood of each nation or each tribe, gradually sinking to the intellectual or religious level of the nation or tribe. ON THE RISE OF A POWER BOTH CONTROLLING AND CONSERVATIVE HUNG, HUMANLY SPEAKING, THE LIFE AND DEATH OF CHRISTIANITY — OF CHRISTIANITY AS A PERMANENT, AGGRESSIVE, EXPANSIVE, AND, TO A CERTAIN EXTENT, UNIFORM SYSTEM. There must be a counterbalance to barbaric force, to the unavoidable anarchy of Teutonism, with its tribal, or at the utmost national, independence, forming a host of small, conflicting, antagonistic kingdoms. . . . *It is impossible to conceive what had been the confusion, the lawlessness, the chaotic state of the Middle Ages without the mediæval Papacy;* and of the mediæval Papacy the real father is Gregory the Great" (*Ib.* Book iii. ch. vii. vol. ii. pp. 100–102).

Speaking of the seventh century, he says :—" It was Christianity alone which maintained some kind of combination among the crumbling fragments of the Roman Empire. . . . Christianity alone was a bond of union, strong and enduring. *The Teutonic kingdoms acknowledged their allegiance to the ecclesiastical supremacy of Rome : Rome was the centre and capital of Western Christendom"* (*Ib.* Book iv. ch. iii. vol. ii. p. 225), " *The Metropolis of Christianity* " (ch. v. p. 299).

After giving an account of the conversion of England, Germany, and other countries by the Missionaries sent by the Popes in the seventh and eighth centuries, he says :—" All these conquests of Christianity were, in a certain sense, the conquests of the Roman See ; . . . reverence for Rome penetrated with the gospel to the remotest parts. Germany was converted to Latin Christianity. Rome was the source, the centre, the regulating authority recognised by the English apostles of the Teutons. The clergy were constantly visiting Rome as the religious capital of the world, to do homage to the head of Western Christendom, to visit the shrines of the Apostles, the more devout to obtain reliques, the more intellectual, knowledge, letters, arts" (*Ib.* ch. vi. p. 307).

" Such was the power of religion in those times, that not merely did it enable the clergy to dictate their policy to armed and powerful sovereigns, to arrest barbarian invasion, and to snatch, as it were, conquests already in their rapacious hands ; in every quarter of Western Europe kings were seen abdicating their thrones, placing themselves at the feet of the Pope as humble penitents, casting off their pomp, and submitting to the privations and the discipline of monks" (*Ib.* Book iv. ch. xi. vol. iii. p. 6).

Speaking of the causes of the degradation of the Papacy in the tenth century, he says :—" In the tenth century the few reflecting minds might not without reason apprehend the approaching dissolution of the world. A vast anarchy seemed to spread over Western Christendom. It is perhaps the darkest period in the history of every country in Europe. The Pagan Magyars, more terrible even than the Islamite Saracens and the Pagan Northmen, now burst upon Europe. . . . The Magyars, or Hungarians, seemed as hordes of savages or of wild beasts let loose upon mankind. They burst unexpectedly upon Christendom in swarms of which the source seemed unknown and inexhaustible. Indiscriminate massacre seemed their only war law ; they were bound by no treaties, respected no boundaries. Civilisation, Christianity, withered before their hosts. . . . They rushed down the Alps ; Italy lay open before them. Splendid Pavia, with its forty-three churches, was in ashes. . . . Rome beheld at no great distance the flame of their devastation ; they spread to the very extremity of the peninsula.[1] . . . The anarchy of Italy led to the degradation of the Papacy" (Book v. ch. xi. vol. iii. pp. 279–282).

" The devout indignation of Baronius as to these times[2] arose no doubt in great part from the severe but honest asceticism of his character, and his horror at this violation of his high notions of sacerdotal sanctity by what appeared to him far more unseemly and unpardonable criminality than arrogance, avarice, or cruelty. His fears, too, lest he should be accused of an immoral partiality by the slightest extenuation, or even by a dispassionate examination of such vices" (of

---

[1] " The Hungarians for half a century were the common terror of Christendom, from their first irruption about A.D. 884 to A.D. 936, the date of the first great victory of Henry the Fowler. Gradually the Magyars settled down within the limits of modern Hungary. At the beginning of the next century Christianity had entirely subdued them, and with a kind of prophetic instinct had arrayed this valiant nation as a future outguard against the Mohammedan Turks ; their King Stephen was a Saint" (MILMAN, *loc. cit.*, p. 280).

[2] Milman is here referring to the very dark picture drawn by Cardinal BARONIUS of the condition of the Papacy in the tenth century.

some of the Popes of that age), "has led him to exaggerate rather than soften the monstrous enormities of these times. And the happy thought, happy in a thoroughgoing controversialist, that the deeper the degradation of the Papacy, the more wonderful, and therefore the more manifestly of God, its restoration to power, removed every remaining repugnance to his abandonment of all the Popes during the tenth century to historical infamy. . . . *Luitprand is the chief, the only authority on which Baronius rests*"[1] (*Ib.* Book v. ch. xi. p. 288, *note*).

Of Pope Leo IX. (A.D. 1054) Milman says :—" Leo came forth to Europe, not only with the power and dignity, but with the austere holiness, the indefatigable religious activity, the majestic virtue, which became the Head of Christendom. . . . In this single spiritual campaign [his religious visitation of Europe], by the calm dignity of his holiness, by his appeal to the strong religious reverence of Christendom, he had restored the Papacy to all its former authority over the minds of men " (*Ib.* Book vi. ch. i. vol. iii. pp. 373, 382).

NEANDER, the German (Protestant) Church historian, speaking of the conflict of the Church with the Empire under Pope Gregory VII. (Hildebrand), says :—

---

[1] This fact is important, inasmuch as the learned MURATORI ("whose accuracy," says HALLAM, "is in general almost implicitly to be trusted, and whose plain integrity speaks in all his writings," *Middle Ages*, ch. iii. p. 1, *note*) charges Luitprand with having "*given credit to all the pasquinades and defamatory libels of the times*" (*Annal.* v. ii. 16, 36, 43, &c.).

" The scandals given by some occupants of the Papal Chair," says a Catholic writer, " are a fruitful theme of reproach, on which Protestants delight to expatiate; yet if we consider the turbulence of the times, the total disorganisation of society, the temporary ascendancy obtained at Rome by some petty potentates, the national partialities which favoured some intruders through jealousy of German influence, we shall not be astonished that in the tenth and eleventh centuries some instances occurred of wicked and ambitious men who seized on the reins of government." In regard to the charges made against various Popes in the same or following centuries, this author observes :—" The character of several Popes has suffered unjustly from the interested misrepresentations of rivals or their partisans, as also of the adherents of schismatical emperors and kings. National jealousies led the Italians to satirise the French Popes who sat at Avignon, while the French viewed with no partiality several who sat at Rome. The civil relations of the Pontiff to his subjects have often cast odium on the exercise of his ecclesiastical authority, and his political associations with various princes have contributed in no slight degree to excite the rancour and provoke the animadversions of writers of other nations. Certain historians assume the air of candour by reciting the very words of some contemporary who has recorded his view of the personal character or public acts of an individual Pope, without reflecting that he may have mistaken rumour for facts, and followed the bias of partisanship to the prejudice of truth and justice. I feel it unnecessary to enter into a detailed vindication of the various Pontiffs whose character is more generally the object of attack ; but I fearlessly say, that considering the long succession of Popes, the convulsions of society, the vicissitudes of Rome, and the endless variety of circumstances in which the Popes have been placed, it is nothing short of a miracle that, in general, their character has been pure and exalted, whilst their succession has been inviolably maintained."

" The great question was . . . whether the system of the Church theocracy, the spiritual universal monarchy, should come off victorious in the contest with a rude secular power, or should be laid prostrate at its feet. . . . The corruption of the Church, threatening its utter secularisation, had now reached its highest pitch, and that very circumstance had called forth a reformatory reaction on the part of the Church. *Such a reaction could, however, under the existing conditions,* ONLY *proceed from the side of this Church Theocracy,*[1] *since those who were most zealous against the abuses that had crept in were governed by this spiritual tendency.* . . . Gregory was certainly inspired with some higher motive than selfish ambition, a selfish love of domination. . . . There were men animated by a warm zeal for the welfare of the Church, and against the deep-rooted abuses of the times, who expected from this imperial sovereignty of the Church, wielded by the Popes, the correction of all evils. . . .

" It was by the degeneracy of the clergy, and the confusion existing in all parts of the Church constitution, that the reforming tendencies of the Hildebrandian epoch had been called forth. A part of the abuses which had crept in, those which the rude arbitrary proceedings of monarchs had introduced, were *thoroughly counteracted by the triumph of the Hildebrandian system; a great zeal for the reformation of the clergy and of the Church life, after the pattern of the primitive Apostolical Church, as it presented itself to the imagination of the men of this period, commenced from this epoch.* A bond of union was here presented between all the opponents of the reigning corruption, all men in all Churches who were zealous for a strict severity of morals among the clergy, and the worthy celebration of the offices of worship. . . . *The Hildebrandian epoch of reform was accompanied with the outpouring of a spirit of compunction and repentance on the Western nations*" (NEANDER'S *Hist. of the Church,* Eng. trans., Bohn's edit., vol. vii. pp. 111, 112, 284, 322).[2]

---

[1] Comp. GUIZOT, Lect. vi. :—"There was within the whole Church but one force adequate to it, and that was the Court of Rome, the Papacy."

[2] That the outpouring of a very different spirit accompanied the *Lutheran* epoch of "reform," will appear from the testimonies hereafter cited.

NEANDER elsewhere speaks of the immense good done by the Monastic Orders, and especially by those monks "who travelled about as preachers of repentance, and who *sided with the Popes* in combating the prevailing corruption of manners and the vicious clergy" (*Ib.* vol. vii. p. 133. See pp. 330, 331, 339, 341 *seq.,* 349 *seq.,* 372–399, &c.). In short, he considers that "to the epochs that mark the commencement of a new outpouring of the Holy Spirit may be reckoned the opening of the twelfth century ; and the after effects of the religious awakening, which then began among the Christian nations of the West, extend far into the period now before us. . . . The religious life was continually receiving a fresh impulse from influences of various kinds : from the vigorous measures of Gregory VII. to promote a reform in the whole Church ; from the impressions produced on the multitude by the preaching of the Crusades; from the effects wrought by distinguished preachers of the clerical, and more especially of the monastic order, who itinerated through the countries, exhorting men to repentance ; from the founding of the two Orders of mendicant friars, &c." (*Ib.* p. 406. See also pp. 483, 484, 492).

Colonel MITCHELL observes :—"*Deep and indelible is the debt which religion and civilisation owe to the early Roman Pontiffs and to the Church of Rome.* They strove long and nobly to forward the cause of human improvement, and it is difficult to say what other power could have exercised so beneficial an influence over the fierce and fiery nations who established themselves on the ruins of the Roman Empire, after rooting out all that remained of ancient art and ancient knowledge. Nor were their efforts confined within these territorial limits : monks and missionaries, disregarding personal danger, penetrated into the forests of Germany and into the distant regions of the North, and, unappalled by the deaths of torture to which so many holy men had fallen victims, preached to heathens and barbarians the mild doctrines of Christianity, which only sprung up in Europe watered by the blood of saints and martyrs. Even the efforts of the Church to interpose its spiritual power in the direction of temporal affairs, and to control the conduct of kings and princes, were beneficial in an age when the clergy alone possessed whatever learning and knowledge were extant ; and the uniformity of belief which rendered all the Western Churches dependent on the authority of the Pope—*an authority so greatly enlightened,* when contrasted with the general darkness of the times—became a principal cause of the progress and prosperity of the Catholic world" (MITCHELL'S *Life of Wallenstein,* pp. 4, 5, edit. 1837).

M. ANCILLON, a French Calvinist, says :—"During the Middle Ages, when there was no social order, *the Papacy alone perhaps saved Europe from utter barbarism.* It created bonds of connection between the most distant nations ; it was a common centre, a rallying-point for isolated states. It was a supreme tribunal established in the midst of universal anarchy ; and its decrees were sometimes as respectable as they were respected ; it prevented and arrested the despotism of the Emperors and diminished the evils of the feudal system" (*Tableau des Revolutions du Système Politique de l'Europe,* vol. i. Introduct., pp. 133, 157).

The German Protestant Church historian STÄUDLEIN says :—
"The Papacy was productive of many beneficial effects. . . . It united in one common bond the different European nations, furthered their mutual intercourse, and became a channel for the communication of the arts and sciences, and without it the fine arts, doubtless, would not have attained to so high a degree of perfection. The Papal power restrained political despotism, and from the rude multitude kept off many of the vices of barbarism" (*Universal Church History,* Hanover, 1806, p. 203).

HERDER, another eminent Protestant writer, says :—
" It is doubtless true that the Roman hierarchy was a necessary power, without which there would have been no check upon the untutored nations of the Middle Ages. Without it, Europe would have fallen under the power of a despot, would have become the theatre of interminable con-

flicts, and have been converted into a Mongolian desert" (*Ideas on the History of Mankind*, Part iv. p. 303. Cf. p. 194 *seq.*)

JOHN VON MÜLLER, the historian of Switzerland, says :—
" All the enlightenment of the present day, whereof the daring spirit of Europe will not allow us to forecast the ultimate consequences, either to ourselves or to the other nations of the world, came originally from that HIERARCHY which, when the Roman Empire fell to pieces, sustained and directed the human race. It imparted, so to speak, to the mind of Northern Europe, which as yet possessed neither elevation nor grasp of thought, a stirring, an energising, and a life-giving impulse, under the impact of which it was carried forward,—retarded indeed by many adverse, and accelerated by some favourable circumstances,—till it finally achieved the triumphs that are now before the world " (*Hist. of Switzerland*, Book iii. ch. i.).

The Rev. E. CUTTS, D.D., in a work published by the Society for Promoting Christian Knowledge, says :—
" In the Middle Ages the Church was *a great popular institution.* . . . One reason, no doubt, of the popularity of the Mediæval Church was that it had always been the champion of the people and the friend of the poor. In politics the Church was always on the side of the liberties of the people against the tyranny of the feudal lords. In the eye of the nobles the labouring population were beings of an inferior caste ; in the eye of the law they were chattels ; in the eye of the Church they were brethren in Christ, souls to be won and trained and fitted for heaven. In social life the Church was an easy landlord and a kind master. . . . On the whole, with many drawbacks, the Mediæval Church did its duty—according to its own light—to the people. It was the great cultivator of learning and art, and it did its best to educate the people. It had vast political influence, and used it on the side of the liberties of the people. . . By means of its painting and sculpture in the churches, its mystery plays, its religious festivals, its catechising and its preaching, it is probable that the chief facts of the Gospel history and the doctrines of the Creeds were more universally known and more vividly realised than among the masses of our present population " (*Turning-Points of English Church History*, 1874, pp. 161-165).

JAMES ANTHONY FROUDE, the historian, says :—
" Never in all their history, in ancient times or modern, never that we know of, have mankind thrown out of themselves anything so grand, so useful, so beautiful as the CATHOLIC CHURCH once was. In these times of ours, well-regulated selfishness is the recognised rule of action—every one of us is expected to look out for first himself, and take care of his own interests. At the time I speak of, the Church ruled the State with the authority of a conscience ; and self-interest, as a motive of action, was only named to be abhorred. The Bishops

and clergy were regarded freely and simply as the immediate ministers of the Almighty; and *they seem to me to have really deserved
that high estimate of their character.* It was not for the doctrines which
they taught, only or chiefly, that they were held in honour. Brave men
do not fall down before their fellow-mortals for the words which they
speak, or for the rites which they perform. Wisdom, justice, self-denial,
nobleness, purity, high-mindedness—these are the qualities before which
the free-born races of Europe have been contented to bow; and *in
no order of men were such qualities to be found as they were found six
hundred years ago in the clergy of the Catholic Church.* They called
themselves the Successors of the Apostles. They claimed, in their
Master's name, universal spiritual authority, but they made good their
pretensions by the holiness of their own lives. They were allowed to rule
because they deserved to rule, and in the fulness of reverence kings and
nobles bent before a power which was nearer to God than their own.
Over prince and subject, chieftain and serf, a body of unarmed defence-
less men reigned supreme by the magic of sanctity. They tamed the
fiery Northern warriors, who had broken in pieces the Roman Empire.
They taught them—they brought them really and truly to believe that
they had immortal souls, and that they would one day stand at the awful
judgment-bar and give account for their lives there. With the brave, the
honest, and the good, with those who had not oppressed the poor nor
removed their neighbour's landmark, with those who had been just in all
their dealings, with those who had fought against evil, and had tried
valiantly to do their Master's will, at that great day it would be well.
For cowards, for profligates, for those who lived for luxury and pleasure
and self-indulgence, there was the blackness of eternal death.

" An awful conviction of this tremendous kind the clergy had effectually
instilled into the mind of Europe. It was not a PERHAPS ; it was a certainty. It was not a form of words repeated once a week at church ; it
was an assurance entertained on all days and in all places, without any
particle of doubt. And the effect of such a belief on life and conscience
was simply immeasurable.

" I do not pretend that the clergy were perfect. They were very far
from perfect at the best of times, and the European nations were never
completely submissive to them. . . . They could not prevent kings from
quarrelling with each other. They could not hinder disputed successions,
and civil feuds, and wars, and political conspiracies. What they did was
to shelter the weak from the strong. In the eyes of the clergy the serf
and his lord stood on the common level of sinful humanity. Into their
ranks high birth was no passport. They were themselves, for the most
part, children of the people ; and the son of the artisan or peasant rose to
the mitre or the triple crown, just as nowadays the railsplitter and the
tailor become Presidents of the Republic of the West. The Church was
essentially democratic while at the same time it had the monopoly of
learning ; and all the secular power fell to it which learning, combined
with sanctity and assisted by superstition, can bestow. . . .

" You have only to look from a distance at any old-fashioned cathedral city, and you will see in a moment the mediæval relations between Church and State. The cathedral *is* the city. The first object you catch sight of as you approach is the spire tapering into the sky, or the huge towers holding possession of the centre of the landscape—majestically beautiful —imposing by mere size amidst the large forms of Nature herself. As you go nearer, the vastness of the building impresses you more and more. The puny dwelling-places of the citizens creep at its feet, the pinnacles are glittering in the tints of the sunset, when down below among the streets and lanes the twilight is darkening. And even now, when the towns are thrice their ancient size, and the houses have stretched upwards from two stories to five ; when the great chimneys are vomiting their smoke among the clouds, and the temples of modern industry—the work-shops and the factories—spread their long fronts before the eye, the cathedral is still the governing form in the picture—the one object which possesses the imagination and refuses to be eclipsed. As that cathedral was to the old town, so was the Church of the Middle Ages to the secular institutions of the world. Its very neighbourhood was sacred ; and its shadow, like the shadow of the Apostles, was a sanctuary " (FROUDE'S *Short Studies on Great Subjects*, vol. i. 2d ed., 1867, pp. 33–37).

Speaking of *one* of the great Religious Orders of the Church, that of ST. BENEDICT, a writer in the DUBLIN UNIVERSITY MAGAZINE says : — " It is a remarkable fact in the history of Christianity, that in its earliest stage—the first phase of its existence—its tendency was to elevate pea-sants to the dignity of Apostles ; but in its second stage it reversed its operations, and brought kings from their thrones to the seclusion of the cloister—humbled the great ones of the earth to the dust of penitential humility. Up to the fourth century, Christianity was a terrible struggle against principalities and powers : then a time came when principalities and powers humbled themselves at the foot of that Cross whose followers they had so cruelly persecuted. The innumerable martyrdoms of the first four centuries of its career were followed by a long succession of royal humiliations,[1] for *during the sixth, seventh, eighth, and ninth centuries, in addition to what took place as regards other Orders, no less than ten emperors and twenty kings resigned their crowns and became monks of the Benedictine Order alone.* . . . Adding to these their subsequent acquisi-tions, *the Benedictines claim, up to the fourteenth century, the honour of enrolling amongst their number twenty emperors and forty-seven kings, twenty sons of emperors and forty-eight sons of kings.* . . . *As nuns of their Order they have had no less than ten empresses and fifty-seven queens. In the wake of these crowned heads follow more than one hundred prin-cesses, daughters of kings and emperors.* . . . The Benedictines produced . . . seven thousand Archbishops, fifteen thousand Bishops, . . . fifteen thousand Abbots, four thousand Saints. They established in different countries altogether thirty-seven thousand monasteries, which sent out

[1] The reader will remember the prophecy in Isai. xlix. 23, &c.

into the world upwards of fifteen thousand seven hundred monks, all of whom attained distinction as authors of books or scientific inventors," &c. (*Dub. Univ. Mag.*, Jan. 1866).

"Western Monasticism, in its general character," says Dean MILMAN, "was not the barren, idly laborious, or dreamy quietude of the East. It was industrious and productive ; it settled colonies, preserved arts and letters, built splendid edifices,[1] fertilised deserts. If it rent from the world the most powerful minds, having trained them by its stern discipline, it sent them back to rule the world. It continually, as it were, renewed its youth, and kept up a constant infusion of vigorous life, now quickening into enthusiasm, now darkening into fanaticism ; and, by its perpetual rivalry, stimulating the zeal or supplying the deficiencies of the secular clergy. In successive ages it adapted itself to the state of the human mind. At first a missionary to barbarous nations, it built abbeys, hewed down forests, cultivated swamps, enclosed domains, retrieved or won for civilisation tracts which had fallen to waste or had never known culture. With St. Dominic it turned its missionary zeal upon Christianity itself, and spread as a preaching Order throughout Christendom ; with St. Francis it became even more popular, and lowered itself to the very humblest of mankind" (*Hist. of Lat. Christ.*, vol. i., Introduct., pp. 7, 8).[2]

D'ISRAELI (the elder) writes :—

[1] "Latin Christianity," says the same writer, "during a period of from ten to twelve centuries, had covered the whole of Western Europe with its still multiplying churches and religious buildings. From the southern shores of Sicily to the Hebrides and the Scandinavian kingdoms, from the doubtful borders of Christian Spain to Hungary, Poland, Prussia, not a city was without its cathedral, surrounded by its succursal churches, its monasteries, and convents, each with its separate church or chapel. There was not a town but above the lowly houses, almost entirely of wood, rose the churches, of stone or some other solid material, in their superior dignity, strength, dimensions, and height ; not a village was without its sacred edifice ; no wayside without its humbler chapel or oratory. Not a river but in its course reflected the towers and pinnacles of many abbeys ; not a forest but above its lofty oaks or pines appeared the long-ridged roof or the countless turrets of the conventual church and buildings. Even now, after periods in some countries of rude religious fanaticism, . . . after the total suppression or great reduction of monastic institutions, the secularisation of their wealth, and the abandonment of their buildings to decay and ruin ; our awe and wonder are still commanded, and seem as if they would be commanded for centuries, by the unshaken solidity, spaciousness, height, majesty, and noble harmony of the cathedrals and churches throughout Western Europe. We are amazed at the imagination displayed in every design, at the enormous human power displayed in their creation ; at the wealth which commanded, the consummate science which guided that power ; at the profound religious zeal which devoted that power, wealth, and science to these high purposes. . . . It is impossible to follow out to their utmost extent, or to appreciate too highly the ennobling, liberalising, humanising, Christianising effects of Church architecture during the Middle Ages " (Book xiv. ch. viii. pp. 268, 289, vol. ix.).

[2] The reader should consult MONTALEMBERT'S splendid work *The Monks of the West*, Eng. trans., 7 vols. 8vo. Comp. the Protestant NEANDER'S *Hist. of the Church*, vol. vii., Bohn's ed., pp. 322 *seq.*, 352 *seq.*, 372 *seq.*, 387, 388, 398, 399, 406, 407.

" It is certainly to the solitary monks that we owe the preservation of the precious remains of ancient literature. We must consider their silent mansions as having afforded the only retreats to science and literature in ages when a universal ignorance threatened to banish from Europe every species of learning. The labour of transcribing books, which then formed one of the chief occupations of the monks, always continued with them, till the discovery of the admirable art of printing. It is thus that all impartial historians dispense only bare justice to the ancient monks, by acknowledging that *it is to their cares and to their labours that we owe the valuable remains of antiquity, as well sacred as profane*" (*Curiosities of Literature*, 1st series, vol. ii. p. 345 *seq.*).

Dr. FARRAR, Canon of Westminster, and Chaplain-in-Ordinary to the Queen, says :—

" What was it that had preserved the best elements of Christianity in the fourth century? The self-sacrifice of the HERMITS. What was it which saved the principles of law, and order, and civilisation? What rescued the wreck of ancient literature from the universal conflagration? What restrained, what converted the inrushing Teutonic races? What kept alive the dying embers of science? What fanned into a flame the white ashes of art? What reclaimed waste lands, cleared forests, drained fens, protected miserable populations, encouraged free labour, equalised widely separated ranks? What was the sole witness for the cause of charity, the sole preservative of even partial education, the sole rampart against intolerable oppression? What force was left which could alone humble the haughty by the courage which is inspired by superiority to those things which most men desire, and elevate the poor by the spectacle of a poverty at once voluntary and powerful? What weak and unarmed power alone retained the strength and the determination to dash down the mailed hand of the baron when it was uplifted against his serf, to proclaim a truce of God between warring violences, and to make insolen wickedness tremble by asserting the inherent supremacy of goodness over transgression, of knowledge over ignorance, of quiet righteousness over brute force? *You will say the Church; you will say Christianity. Yes, but for many a long century the very bulwarks and ramparts of the Church were the monasteries, and the one invincible force of the Church lay in the self-sacrifice, the holiness, the courage of the* MONKS " (*Saintly Workers*, pp. 82, 83, ed. 1878).

" From the fifth to the thirteenth century," says the same writer, " the Church was engaged in elaborating the most splendid organisation which the world has ever seen. Starting with the separation of the spiritual from the temporal power, and the mutual independence of each in its own sphere, Catholicism worked hand in hand with feudalism for the amelioration of mankind. Under the influence of feudalism slavery became serfdom, and aggressive was modified into defensive war.[1] Under the

---

[1] M. GUIZOT says :—" There can be no doubt that the Church struggled resolutely against the great vices of the social state,—against slavery, for instance ;

D

influence of Catholicism the monasteries preserved learning and maintained the sense of the unity of Christendom. Under the combined influence of both grew up the lovely ideal of chivalry, moulding generous instincts into gallant institutions, making the body vigorous and the soul pure, and wedding the Christian virtues of humility and tenderness to the natural graces of courtesy and strength. *During this period the Church was the one mighty witness for light in an age of darkness, for order in an age of lawlessness, for personal holiness in an epoch of licentious rage.* Amid the despotism of kings and the turbulence of aristocracies, it was an inestimable blessing that there should be a power which, by the unarmed majesty of simple goodness, made the haughtiest and the boldest respect the interests of justice, and tremble at the thought of temperance, righteousness, and the judgment to come" (Farrar's *Hulsean Lectures* for 1870, p. 115, Lect. iii., *The Victories of Christianity*).

" Once more, consider what the Church did for *Education.* Her ten thousand monasteries kept alive and transmitted that torch of learning which otherwise would have been extinguished long before. A religious education, incomparably superior to the mere athleticism of the noble's hall, was extended to the meanest serf who wished for it. This fact alone, by proclaiming the dignity of the Individual, elevated the entire hopes and destinies of the race. The humanising machinery of Schools and Universities, the civilising propaganda of missionary zeal, were they not due to her ? And, more than this, her very existence was a living education ; it showed that the successive ages were not sporadic and accidental scenes, but were continuous and coherent acts in the one great drama. In Christendom the yearnings of the past were fulfilled, the direction of the future determined. In dim but magnificent procession, 'the giant forms of empires on their way to ruin' had each ceded to *her* their sceptres, bequeathed to *her* their gifts. . . . Life became one broad rejoicing river, whose tributaries, once severed, were now united, and whose majestic stream, without one break in its continuity, flowed on, under the common sunlight, from its Source beneath the Throne of God" (*Ib.* p. 186, Lect. v., *Christianity and the Race*).

Mr. LECKY observes that :—

" The Catholic Church was the very heart of Christendom, and the spirit that radiated from her penetrated into all the relations of life, and coloured the institutions it did not create. . . . A certain unity of type was then manifested, which has never been restored. . . . This ascendancy was gained by mediæval Catholicity more completely than by any other

. . . Lastly, she strove by all sorts of means to restrain violence and continued warfare in society. Every one knows what was the *Truce of God,* and numerous measures of a similar kind, by which the Church struggled against the employment of force, and strove to introduce more order and gentleness into society. These facts are so well known that it is needless for me to enter into details " (*Hist. of Civilisat.*, Lect. vi.). Comp. BALMEZ, *European Civilisat.*, Eng. trans., p. 66 *et seq.*

system before or since, and the stage of civilisation that resulted from it was one of the most important in the evolutions of society. By consolidating the heterogeneous and anarchical elements that succeeded the downfall of the Roman Empire, by infusing into Christendom the conception of a bond of unity that is superior to the divisions of nationhood, and of a moral tie that is superior to force, by softening slavery into serfdom and preparing the way for the ultimate emancipation of labour, *Catholicism laid the very foundations of modern civilisation.* Herself the most admirable of all organisations, there were formed beneath her influence a vast network of organisations, political, municipal, and social, which supplied a large proportion of the materials of almost every modern structure. . . . In the transition from slavery to serfdom, and in the transition from serfdom to liberty, she was the most zealous, the most unwearied, and the most efficient agent " (*Hist. of Rationalism*, vol. ii. pp. 36, 37, 209).

Dr. MAITLAND declares that :—

" At the darkest periods the Christian Church was the source and spring of civilisation, the dispenser of what little comfort and security there was in the things of this world, and the quiet scriptural asserter of the rights of man " (*Essays on the Dark Ages*, p. 393).

Regarding the charges of ignorance and corruption of morals, alleged against the mediæval clergy and monks, he says :—

" There were in the dark ages (as well as at other times) two sets of persons, from whose writings it is easy to cull passages describing ' the clergy ' as less learned and religious than they were bound to be ; and each set tempted to detail, and perhaps to exaggerate, the vices of ecclesiastics. First, there were those who hated the religion which the clergy maintained, and who envied the property, privileges, and influence which they enjoyed,[1] and which (whatever the personal character of some of them might be) they generally employed to check the licentiousness of others. Among these there have perhaps always been facetious persons who have considered religion and its ministers as fit subjects for their drollery, and who have delighted to represent the clergy as a vile race of knaves and fools, characterised only by pride, sensuality, avarice, and ambition, except where all these, and all that was better, was kept under by idiot superstition. . . . The second set of writers to whom I have alluded are those who, either under pretence, or with the real object, of producing reformation, have been vigilant to spy out, and forward to publish, the vices of Churchmen.[2] . . . From both these sets of writers

---

[1] The untenability or utter falsity of most of the charges made against the Religious Houses of this country in the reign of Henry VIII. has been recently more fully exposed by Dr. DIXON, Protestant Canon of Carlisle, in vol. i. of his *Hist. of the Church of England from the Abolition of the Roman Jurisdiction.* In this work many of Mr. FROUDE'S statements are refuted.

[2] The Spanish historian BALMEZ, after admitting " that lamentable abuses had crept in during the course of the Middle Ages, that the corruption of morals had

very strong statements may be extracted, and the testimony which they apparently give will seem, to the young student of ecclesiastical history, to be confirmed by the proceedings of Councils and the tenor.of their canons, as well as by a good deal of what he will find in the works of secular historians, even supposing that he does go to the original sources. He must, however, remember that sin, in some shape or other, is the great staple of history and the sole object of law; and he must expect, from both the historian and the legislator, to hear more of one turbulent prelate, or one set of factious or licentious monks, than of a hundred societies or a thousand scattered clergy living in the quiet decency suited to their profession " (*Ib.* p. 33).

Mr. EDMUND FFOULKES, writes :—

" As little can it be denied that the glories of the thirteenth century were due to the vigorous reforms inaugurated by St. Gregory VII. and his successors, as that the fourteenth and fifteenth centuries witnessed a very extensive declension of manners and discipline, though by no means of civilisation. Even on the former head, were I writing a Church history, there would be some extenuating circumstances to be produced in behalf of a period during which upwards of fifty Universities [1] were founded in

been great, and that consequent reform was required; " and after showing that these abuses were to be attributed to "the evils of the time alone," continues :— "But were the spirit and ardent desire of reforming abuses ever wanting in the Church ? It can be shown that they were not. I will not mention the Saints whom she did not cease to produce during these unhappy periods ; history proves their number and their virtues, which, so vividly contrasting with the corruption of the age, show that the divine flames which descended on the Apostles had not been extinguished in the bosom of the Catholic Church. This fact proves much ; but there is another still more remarkable—a fact less subject to dispute, and which we cannot be accused of exaggerating—a fact which is not limited to individuals, but which is, on the contrary, the most complete expression of the spirit by which the whole body of the Church was animated ; I mean, *the constant meeting of Councils, in which abuses were reproved and condemned, and in which sanctity of morals and the observance of discipline were continually inculcated.* Happily this consoling fact is indisputable ; it is open to every eye ; and to be aware of it one only needs consult a volume of ecclesiastical history on the proceedings of Councils. . . . Simony and incontinence were the prevailing vices : if you open the canons of Councils, you will find them everywhere anathematised. . . ." (See BALMEZ on *European Civilisation, Protestantism and Catholicity Compared,* 3d Eng. edit., p. 8 *seq.* and p. 400).

[1] The German historian ALZOG says that "*sixty-six* Universities, of which sixteen belonged to Germany, existed in Europe before the year 1517 " (*Universal Church Hist.,* Eng. trans., ed. Gill, Dublin, 1880, vol. iii. p. 179). The principal of these were the Universities of Paris, Bologna, and Salerno (see the Prot. Church historian MOSHEIM, Maclaine's edit., vol. iii. p. 28 *et seq.*). A complete list of them, with the dates of their foundation, is given by ALZOG (vol. ii. p. 523 *note*). The number in *Italy* was sixteen ; in *France,* thirteen ; in *Portugal* and

all parts of Europe ; gorgeous Cathedrals of the stamp of Orvieto, Sienna, Milan, Strasburg, Winchester (as restored by William of Wykeham), Toledo, and Seville erected ; professorial chairs for the study of Hebrew and Chaldee, Greek and Arabic, ordained by a General Council for Rome, Paris, Oxford, Bologna, and Salamanca. No less than twenty printed editions of the Bible were brought out in High or Low Germany alone[1] between A.D. 1460 and the age of Luther ; upwards of 1200 books issued from the printing presses of Italy alone between A.D. 1471-80.[2] For commentators on the Bible, it could boast of Tostatus and Nicholas of Lyra ; for masters of the inner life, John Tauler and Thomas à Kempis ; for ideal artists, Fra Angelico and Fra Bartolomeo. It was not behind-hand in men and women of the saintly graces of St. Catherine of Sienna, St. Bridget, St. Elizabeth of Portugal, St. Vincent Ferrier, and St. John Cantius ; of the ardent philanthropy of Bartholomew de las Casas ; of the splendid abilities of Cardinal Ximenes, or the splendid munificence of William of Wykeham and Wainflete" (*Christendom's Divisions*, vol. i. p. 130).

Regarding the Council of Trent, HALLAM says :—
"It is usual for Protestant writers to inveigh against the Tridentine Fathers. I do not assent to their decisions, which is not to the purpose ; . . . but I must presume to say, that reading their proceedings in the pages of that very able and not very lenient historian to whom we have generally recourse, an adversary as decided as any that could have come from the Reformed Churches,[3] I find proofs of much ability, considering the embarrassments with which they had to struggle, and of an honest desire of reformation among a large body as to those matters which in their judgment ought to be reformed" (*Hist. of Literat. of Europe*, part i. ch. vi. sect. 25 *note* ; vol. i. p. 376; ed. 1860). And again :—" No General Council ever contained *so many persons of eminent learning and ability* as that of Trent ; nor is there ground for believing that any other ever investigated the questions before it with so much patience, acuteness,

Spain, eleven ; in *England*, two ; in *Scotland*, three ; in *Burgundy*, one ; in *Brabant*, one ; in *Germany*, sixteen ; in *Bohemia*, one ; in *Poland*, one ; in *Denmark*, one ; in *Sweden*, one ; in *Hungary*, three ; in *Ireland*, one.

[1] See ALZOG, vol. iii. p. 142 (he is speaking of Bibles in the German language).

[2] HALLAM says :—" The books printed in Italy during these ten years amount, according to Panzer, to 1297, of which 234 are editions of ancient classical authors. Books without date are of course not included ; and the list must not be reckoned complete as to others" (*Hist. of Literature of Europe*, part i. ch. iii. n. 44).

[3] Of Paul Sarpi's *Hist. of the Council of Trent* HALLAM elsewhere says :—"It became the text-book of Protestantism on the subject. . . . It appears to me quite out of doubt . . . that he was *entirely hostile to the Church*, in the usual sense, as well as to the Court of Rome, *sympathising in affection and concurring generally in opinion with the Reformed denomination*" (*Hist. of Literat.*, part iii. ch. ii. sect. 3 ; vol. ii. p. 398). Sarpi's errors and misrepresentations were exposed by Cardinal PALLAVICINO in his authentic *History of the Council of Trent*.

temper, and desire of truth" (*Ib.* part ii. ch. ii. sect. 18 *note ;* vol. ii. p. 71 *note*). Regarding the labours of the Popes and of the Catholic Church at this period for the *reformation of morals*, &c., see also RANKE'S *Hist. of the Popes*, Bohn's edit., vol. i. pp. 110, 214, 233, 249, 264, 265, &c. Comp. vol. ii. pp. 160, 179, 182 *seq.*

"*Ancient Christianity.*"

Dr. ISAAC TAYLOR, a well-known Protestant writer, says :—
"No reader of Church history can require it to be proved that the various rites and usages on account of which the Romish and Greek Churches are usually impugned as idolatrous by Protestants, were openly practised and were authorised by the heads of the Church in the age of Gregory I. But when did these superstitions first make their appearance? It is superfluous to produce evidence of their existence and prevalence in the times immediately preceding those of Pope Gregory. Gregory of Tours, Leo I., Evagrius, Sozomen, Socrates, Theodoret, Isidore, Cyril of Alexandria, and many others, forbid the supposition that they, or any of their contemporaries, had been the *authors* of the opinions or the usages now in question. The men of that period did indeed give their superstitions a more distinct expression, and in various instances they amplified particular rites ; yet only as a man clears, and plants, and beautifies an inheritance on which his ancestors had toiled in like manner" (*Ancient Christianity*, vol. ii. p. 173, 1842).

In p. 92 he speaks of—" 1. Chrysostom's personal and cordial approval of demonolatrous [Saint and Martyr] worship. 2. The UNIVERSALITY of these superstitions, or the fact that the Christianised people of the *fourth* century practised, in these respects, *whatever is now characteristic of the Greek and Romish communions.* 3. These practices were *not then of recent origin.*" [1]

After filling about forty pages of his work with citations from Basil, Ephræm Syrus, Gregory Nazianzen, Chrysostom, Asterius, and others, he says :—

"*Not a fiftieth part* of what might deserve to be called *the evidence* bearing upon our subject has been produced. *Scarcely a writer, if there be one, of the Nicene Church—Eastern or Western—would withhold his contributions to the mass; and alas! what a volume would Augustine alone furnish!* . . . The few passages that have been cited will, I think, be enough to satisfy every honest and intelligent reader as to the broad fact assumed—viz., that the direct invocation of Saints and Martyrs, and an idolatrous veneration of their symbols and relics, were *carried to as culpable an extreme in the Nicene Church as they have at any time since been carried in the Romish Church;* and that in whatever terms we may choose to express our disapprobation of those superstitions as practised

---

[1] Dr. LITTLEDALE has the assurance to affirm that "we find *the first germs* of the practice (of the Invocation of Saints) *at the close of the fourth century ;*" and he refers to St. Chrysostom as being opposed to the same ! (*Plain Reasons, &c.*, 3d edit., p. 34).

by the latter, they cannot, with any colour of reason, be retracted when we have to speak of the same as attaching to the former" (*Ib.* pp. 213, 214).

With respect to St. Ambrose, he says :—" A Romanist might proceed to argue :—Most distinctly does he recognise and authenticate Prayers for the dead—Prayers to the dead—the merit of Penance—the Supremacy of the Bishop of Rome—and that opinion of the miraculous property of the Eucharistic elements which Protestants deny. Is it equitable, then, in argument, to quote this Father *against* Romanists, when in truth his testimony, taken as a whole, bears most decisively against Protestantism? *Such a reply can by no means be rebutted*" (Supplement, p. 19). "In almost every instance in which Protestants and Romanists are at issue, Ambrose may properly be appealed to by the latter, and not the former" (*Ib.* p. 37). "Augustine allows and recommends all that the Church of Rome formally sanctions ; or, at the least, he authorises that which all Protestants utterly condemn" (*Ib.* p. 25).

The Bible in the Church.

The Rev. E. CUTTS, D.D., in a work published by the Society for Promoting Christian Knowledge, says :—

"There is a good deal of popular misapprehension about the way in which the Bible was regarded in the Middle Ages. Some people think that it was very little read, even by the clergy ; whereas the fact is that the sermons of the mediæval preachers are more full of Scripture quotations and allusions than any sermons in these days ; and the writers on other subjects are so full of Scriptural allusion, that it is evident their minds were saturated with Scriptural diction. . . . Another common error is, that the clergy were unwilling that the laity should read the Bible for themselves, and carefully kept it in an unknown tongue, that the people might not be able to read it. The truth is, that most people who could read at all could read Latin, and would certainly prefer to read the authorised Vulgate to any vernacular version. But it is also true that translations into the vernacular were made. . . . We have the authority of Sir Thomas More for saying that 'the whole Bible was, long before Wycliffe's days, by virtuous and well-learned men, translated into the English tongue, and by good and godly people with devotion and soberness well and reverently read.' . . . Again, on another occasion, he says : —'The clergy keep no Bibles from the laity but such translations as be either not yet approved for good, or such as be already reproved for naught (bad), as Wycliffe's was. For as for old ones that were before Wycliffe's days, they remain lawful, and be in some folk's hands'" (*Turning-Points of English Church History*, 1874, pp. 200, 201).

The QUARTERLY REVIEW (October 1879) says :—

"The notion that people in the Middle Ages did not read their Bibles is probably exploded, except among the more ignorant of controversialists. But a glance at this volume (Dean Goulburn's *Life of Bishop Herbert de Losinga*) is enough to show that *the notion is not simply a mistake—that it is one of the most ludicrous and grotesque of blunders. If having the Bible at their fingers' ends could have saved the Middle Age teachers from abuses and false doctrine, they were certainly well equipped.* They were not merely accomplished textuaries. They had their minds as saturated with the language and associations of the sacred text as the Puritans of the seventeenth century." (See also MAITLAND'S *Dark Ages*, pp. 220, 221, 470.)

Early Printed Catholic Versions of the Bible.

I. LATIN BIBLES.—The Protestant essàyist on "THE DARK AGES," when refuting D'Aubigné's absurd statement that the Bible was "*a rare book, unknown in those days*," when Luther "discovered" a copy of a Latin Bible in the monastery at Erfurt, says :—" To say nothing of *parts* of the Bible, or of books whose *place* is uncertain, we know of, at least, *twenty different editions of the whole Latin Bible, printed in Germany only before Luther was born.*" In addition to these :—" *Before Luther was born* the Bible had been printed in Rome, Naples, Florence, and Placenza, and Venice alone had furnished eleven editions." " No doubt," he adds, " we should be within the truth if we were to say that beside the multitude of manuscript copies, not yet fallen into disuse, the *press* had issued *fifty* different editions of the whole Latin Bible, to say nothing of Psalters, New Testaments, and other parts " (MAITLAND'S *Essays on the Dark Ages*, p. 469).

This estimate is, however, very far within the truth. REUSS, a leading Rationalist of Germany, says that "no book was so frequently published immediately after the first invention of printing as the Latin Bible, more than one hundred editions of it being struck off before the year 1520" (Ed. Reuss, *Die Geschichte der heiligen schriften, N. T.*, Brunswick, 1853, p. 458). HAIN, in his *Repertorium Bibliographicum*, printed at Tubingen, reckons consecutively *ninety-eight distinct editions before the year* 1500, independently of *twelve other editions*, which, together with the Latin text, presented the Glossa Ordinaria, or the Postillas of Lyranus. From the year 1475, when the first Venetian edition appeared, to the close of the century, that city yielded no fewer than *twenty-two complete editions* of the Latin Bible, besides some others with the notes of Lyranus. (See *Irish Ecclesiast. Record*, vol. i. p. 255.)

II. GERMAN BIBLES.[1]—The first German printed Bible, bearing the arms of Frederick III., issued from the Mentz press about 1462. Another version appeared in 1466, two copies of which are still preserved in the

---

[1] The CHURCH TIMES of July 26, 1878, speaking of the *List of Bibles in the Caxton Exhibition* (South Kensington, 1877), published by H. Stevens, says :— " This catalogue will be very useful for one thing, at any rate, as disproving the popular lie about Luther's *finding* the Bible for the first time at Erfurt about 1507. Not only are there very many editions of the Latin Vulgate long anterior to that time, but *there were actually nine* GERMAN *editions of the Bible in the Caxton Exhibition earlier than* 1483, *the year of Luther's birth,* and at least three more before the end of the century."

Senatorial Library at Leipsic. Other versions were published in rapid succession.[1]

III. ITALIAN BIBLES.—Three editions of the Bible in the Italian tongue appeared in the year 1471, one being a translation by Nicholas Malermi, a Camaldolese monk, and the two others by writers of the fourteenth century. No fewer than *eleven* complete editions of these several versions appeared before the year 1500, and were reprinted *eight* times more before the year 1567, *with the express permission of the " Holy Office."* More than forty editions are reckoned before the appearance of the first Protestant version in Italian. An entirely new translation was made by Sanctes Marmoschini in 1538, and was reprinted in 1546. Another by Bruccioli of Venice in 1532, from which date to 1552, *twelve* editions of this version appeared ; but though remarkable for its Tuscan dialect, it was inaccurate in many passages, and for this reason was condemned by the ecclesiastical authorities. The first *Protestant* Italian Bible was printed at Geneva in 1562, and was little more than a reprint of Bruccioli's version.

IV. SPANISH BIBLES.—In Spain the whole Bible, which had been translated into the vernacular tongue by Boniface Ferrier in 1405, was printed in 1478, and reprinted in 1515, *with the formal consent of the Spanish Inquisition.* In 1512, the Gospels and Epistles were translated by Ambrosio Montesma, and this work was republished at Antwerp in 1544 ; at Barcelona in 1601 and 1608 ; and at Madrid in 1603 and 1615. CARRANZA, the celebrated Archbishop of Toledo, says in the Prologue to his Commentaries :—" Before the heresies of Luther appeared, I do not know that the Holy Scriptures in the vulgar tongue were anywhere forbidden. In Spain, the Bible was translated into it by order of the Catholic sovereigns, at the time when the Moors and Jews were allowed to live among the Christians according to their own law." He then proceeds to show why the *indiscriminate circulation* of the same (from which so much evil naturally resulted) was subsequently prohibited in Spain. (See BALMEZ *On European Civilisat.*, ch. xxxvi., Eng. trans., p. 192.)

V. FRENCH BIBLES.—A French translation of the New Testament, by two Augustinian friars, Julian Macho and Pierre Farget, was published at Lyons in 1478. A copy of this version is preserved in the public library of Leipsic. The version of De Moulins appeared soon afterwards in a

---

[1] They appeared as follows :—At Mayence in 1467 ; Nuremburg, 1477, 1483, 1490, 1518; Augsburg, 1477, 1480, 1483, 1487, 1490, 1494, 1507, 1518, 1524 ; Strasburg, 1485. Fust's edition was printed in 1472. Seckendorf speaks of three other distinct versions of the German Bible, printed at Wittemberg in 1470, 1483, and 1490 (*Comment. in Lutheran.*, lib. i. sect. 51). Versions in other dialects appeared at Lubeck in 1494, at Halberstadt in 1522, at Cologne between 1470 and 1480, at Delft in 1477, at Gouda in 1479, at Louvain in 1518. (See PANZER's *List of all the Bibles Printed in Old German*, Nuremburg, 1774, and the *New History of Catholic German Bibles*, Nuremburg, 1784.)

quarto edition, and a new edition, carefully revised by Jean de Rely, was published in Paris under the auspices of Charles VIII. in 1487. It passed through *fourteen* other editions in Paris and Lyons alone, before the year 1546. Menaud's version was published in 1484, and that of James le Fevre in 1512. This last, corrected by the Louvain divines, became so popular that it passed through more than forty editions before the year 1700. Another French Catholic translation, by Nicholas de Leuse, was printed at Antwerp in 1534. The first *Protestant* version was printed at Neufchatel in 1535.

VI. OTHER VERSIONS.—Amongst these may be mentioned particularly the FLEMISH translation made by Jacobus Merland, cir. A.D. 1210, which was printed at Cologne in 1475, and passed through *seven* editions before the year 1530, and of which the Antwerp edition was republished *eight* times in the space of seventeen years; the Flemish translation of the New Testament by Cornelius Kendrick, 1524, of which *ten* editions were published at Antwerp alone within thirty years; a BOHEMIAN version published at Prague in 1488, at Cutra in 1498, and at Venice in 1506 and 1511; a SCLAVONIAN at Cracow; and an ETHIOPIC Bible at Rome in 1548, &c.

Complete lists of the various Catholic translations of the Bible will be found in LE LONG's *Bibliotheca Sacra*, 2 vols. fol., Paris, 1723; and in the *Bibliothèque Curieuse* of the Calvinist writer, DAVID CLEMENT, 9 vols. 4to, Gottingen, 1750. See also the first seven vols. of Panzer's *Annales Typographici* (Nuremburg, 1791-1803), the *Dublin Review*, vol. i., and the *Irish Ecclesiastical Record*, vol. i.

Of the celebrated "COMPLUTENSIAN POLYGLOT" of Cardinal Ximenes (published in 6 vols. fol., 1515), and of the early Catholic editions of the HEBREW and GREEK Scriptures, it is unnecessary here to speak.

The English and Foreign "Reformation"—Its early Effects on Christian Faith and Morals, as described by the Reformers themselves and by later Protestant Historians.

I. ITS EFFECTS ON CHRISTIAN BELIEF.

CALVIN, writing to Melanchthon, says :—"It is of great importance that *the divisions* which subsist amongst us should not be known to future ages; for nothing can be more ridiculous than that we, who have been obliged to separate from the whole world (a toto mundo discessionem facere coacti sumus), should have agreed so ill among ourselves from the very beginning of the Reformation" (*Epist.* 141).

BEZA writes to Dudith :—" I have also been long and greatly tormented by the same thoughts which you describe to me. I see our people wander at the mercy of every wind of doctrine, and after having been raised up, fall, sometimes on one side and sometimes on the other. What they think of religion to-day you may know ; what they will think of it to-morrow you cannot affirm. *On what point of religion are the Churches which have declared war against the Pope agreed amongst themselves? Examine all, from beginning to the end; you will hardly find one thing affirmed by the one which the other does not directly cry out against as impiety* " (In quo tandem religionis capite congruunt inter se ecclesiæ, quæ Romano Pontifici bellum indixerunt? A capite ad calcem si per-curras omnia, nihil propemodum reperias ab uno affirmari, quod alter statim non impium esse clamitet.—*Epist ad And. Dudit.*, ap. BALMEZ, *European Civilisat.*, p. 402).

MELANCHTHON declared that "the Elbe with all its waters could not furnish tears enough to weep over *the miseries of the distracted Refor-mation*" (*Epis.* 202, lib. ii.). See also BOSSUET'S *Hist. of the Varia-tions of the Protestant Churches*, bk. v. ch. iv., and bk. ii. ch. xliii.

HALLAM says :—"We ought to reckon among the principal causes of this change [the decline of Protestantism and the Catholic reaction in the latter half of the sixteenth century] *those perpetual disputes, those irre-concilable animosities, that bigotry above all, and persecuting spirit, which were exhibited in the Lutheran and Calvinistic Churches*" (*Hist. of Literature of Europe*, part ii. ch. ii. sect. 20; vol. ii. ed. 1860, p. 73). " Thus, in the second period of the Reformation, those ominous symptoms which had appeared in its earlier stage, disunion, virulence, bigotry, intolerance, *far from yielding to any benignant influence, grew more inveterate and incurable*" (*Ib.* sect. 29, p. 80).

Speaking of the learned Protestant GROTIUS, he says :—" The ill-usage he sustained at the hands of those who boasted their independence of Papal tyranny, the caresses of the Gallican clergy after he had fixed his residence in Paris, *the growing dissensions and virulence of the Protestants, the choice that seemed alone to be left in their communion between fanatical anarchy, disintegrating everything like a Church, on the one hand, and a domination of vulgar and bigoted ecclesiastics on the other*, made him gradually less and less averse to the COMPREHENSIVE AND MAJESTIC UNITY OF THE CATHOLIC HIERARCHY, and more and more disposed to concede some point of uncertain doctrine or some form of ambiguous expression " (*Ib.* part iii. ch. ii. sect. 13 ; vol. ii. p. 409).

For a full account of the ANGLICAN SCHISM, and of the variations in doctrine of the " Church as by Law Established," the reader may be referred to the Rev. W. WATERWORTH's *Orgin and Development of Angli-canism* (Burns & Oates) ; and he may also advantageously consult the *History of the Church of England, from the Abolition of the Roman Jurisdiction*, by Dr. DIXON, Protestant Canon of Carlisle.

About the middle of the seventeenth century, Dr. WALTON, the editor of the celebrated Polyglot Bible, in six volumes folio, and afterwards Bishop of Chester, writes :—"Aristarchus formerly could hardly find seven wise men in Greece ; but amongst us [English] are hardly to be found so many ignorant persons; for all are teachers, all divinely instructed There is no fanatic or clown, from the lowest dregs of the people, who does not give you his own dreams for the word of God. For the bottomless pit seems to have been set open, from whence a smoke has risen which has obscured the heavens and the stars, and locusts are come out with stings, a numerous race of sectaries and heretics, who have renewed all the old heresies, and invented monstrous opinions of their own. These have filled our cities, villages, camps, houses ; nay, our churches and pulpits too, and lead the poor deluded people with them to the pit of perdition" (*Pref. ad Proleg. in Bibl. Polyglotta*, ed. Cambridge, 1828).

II. ITS EFFECTS ON MORALS.

Protestant writers can gain nothing by exaggerating, as they commonly do, the evils and corruption of morals that existed *before* the time of the so-called Reformation, seeing that according to the unanimous testimony of the Reformers themselves, and of all truthful historians, matters became much worse wherever their new gospel was spread, and amongst the majority of those who embraced it.

LUTHER himself declared :—" The world grows worse from day to day. *Men are now much more covetous, malicious, and resentful, much more unruly, shameless, and full of vice, than they were in the time of Popery* " (Mundus in dies fit deterior. Sunt nunc homines magis vindictæ cupidi, magis avari, magis ab omni misericordia remoti, magis immodesti et indisciplinati, multoque deteriores quam fuerint in Papatu.—*In Postill. super Evang. Dominicæ primæ Advent.*).

" Formerly, when we were seduced by the Pope, men willingly followed good works ; but *now* all their study is to get everything to themselves, by exactions, pillage, theft, lying, and usury " (*Serm. Dom. 26 post Trinit.*).

"With regard to our Germany, it is evident, according to the great light of the Gospel, that it is clean possessed by the devil. Our youths are impudent and unruly, and will no longer submit to education ; the old men are loaded with sins of avarice, usury, and many others that may not be told " (Luth. *in Gen.* xxiii. 9, tom. i. p. 2451).

CALVIN says :—" When so many thousand men, having thrown off the Papal authority, eagerly enrolled themselves under the Gospel, how few, think you, have repented of their vices ? Nay, what has *the majority* shown to have been their desire, than that, having shaken off the yoke of superstition, they might launch out the more freely into every kind of lasciviousness ? " (Ut excusso superstitionum jugo, solutius in omnem lasciviam diffluerent.—*De Scandalis*, tom. ix. p. 71, ed. Amstelod, 1667).

WILIBALD PIRCKHEIMER,[1] A.D. 1528 :—" O splendid Christianity ! I

---

[1] HALLAM says :—" Munzer and Knipperdoling, with the whole brood of Anabaptist fanatics, were the legitimate brood of Luther's early doctrine. And

know, and it is the truth, that even unbelievers were not guilty of such fraud and crime as these who call themselves 'Evangelicals.' For the fact is evident to be seen, that there is now neither faith nor hope, no fear of God, no love of one's neighbour ; but there is a rejection of mercy and goodness, of art and of learning ; nor do they now think of aught save the gratification of the body," &c. (*Epist. to Tscherte*, in *Reliquien von Albrecht Durer*, Nuremberg, 1828, p. 168).

BUCER, a prominent " Reformer," also says :—" The *greater part* of the people seem only to have embraced the gospel in order to shake off the yoke of discipline and the obligation of fasting, penance, &c., which lay upon them in Popery, and to live at their pleasure, enjoying their lusts and lawless appetites without control. *Hence* they lend a willing ear to the doctrine that we are saved by faith alone, and not by works, having no relish for them " (*De Regno Christi*, lib. i. c. 4).

ERASMUS wrote, after sufficient experience of the "Reformation : "— " Look around on this 'Evangelical' people, and observe whether there be less luxury, debauchery, and avarice amongst them than among those you so hate. Show me any one whom that new gospel has changed from a drunkard to a sober man, from a cruel to a gentle, from a greedy to a liberal, from a malignant to an amiable, from an impure to a chaste one. *I will show you many who have become worse through following it*" (Circumspice populum illum evangelicum ; . . . et profer mihi quem istud evangelium ex commessatore sobrium, ex feroci mansuetum, ex rapaci liberalem, ex maledico benedicum, ex impudico redidderit verecundum. Ego tibi multos ostendam qui facti sunt seipsis deteriores.—*Epist. ad Vulturium Neocomum*).

" Those whom I had once known to be chaste, sincere, and without fraud, I found, *after they had embraced this sect*, to be licentious in their conversation, gamblers, neglectful of prayer, passionate, vain, as spiteful as serpents, and lost to the feelings of human nature. I speak from experience " (Quos antea noveram puros, candidos, et fuci ignaros, eosdem vidi, ubi sectæ se dedissent, loqui cæpissime de puellis, luisse alcam, abjecisse preces, impatientissimos omnis injuriæ, vanos, viperinos

even if we set these aside, *it is certain that we find no testimonies to any reform of manners in the countries that embraced it*. . . . This great practical deficiency in the Lutheran reformation is confessed by their own writers. And it is attested by a remarkable letter of Wilibald Pirckheimer, announcing the death of Albert Durer to a correspondent at Vienna in 1528. . . . In this he takes occasion to inveigh against the bad conduct of the Reformed party at Nuremberg, and seems as indignant at the Lutherans as he had ever been against Popery, though without losing his hatred for the latter. . . . The witness he bears to the dishonest and dissolute manners which had accompanied the introduction of Lutheranism is not to be slightly regarded, considering 'the respectability of Pirckheimer, and his known co-operation with the first reform " (*Hist. of Literat. of Europe*, part i. ch. iv. sect. 60 *note*, 6th ed.).

in moribus, ac prorsus hominem exuisse. Expertus loquor.—*Epist. ad Fratres Infer. Germaniæ*, Colon., 1561).

"The letters of Erasmus," says HALLAM, "are a perpetual commentary on the mischiefs with which the Reformation, in his opinion, was accompanied" (*Hist. of Literat. of Europe*, pt. i. ch. vi. sect. 8, *note*; vol. i. p. 361).

Mr. BARING GOULD (an Anglican) says :—" Even in Luther's time the proclamation of free justification by faith only led to grave disorders, and frightened back into Catholicism many who wished the Reformation success. One instance alone will serve to show the results of the doctrine of Solifidianism. In Ditmarchen, Neocorus tells us, chastity and innocence were so remarkable, that the little principality went by the name of the Land of Mary. In 1532 it was Lutheranised. Nine years after, in 1541, the Reformer Nicholas Boje complained that 'fornication, adultery, and usury were practised in a way unusual even among Jews and heathens, and had so gained the upper-hand that it was impossible to supply any remedy by sermons.' . . .
" There is abundant evidence to show that *wherever the Reformation in Germany prevailed, the moral tone sank several degrees*" (BARING GOULD'S *Germany, Past and Present*, vol. ii. pp. 175–178, Lond. 1879).

As regards our own country, KING HENRY VIII. declared, in his last speech to Parliament :—" The Bible itself is turned into wretched rhymes, sung and jangled in every alehouse and tavern. *I am sure that charity was never so faint among ye, virtue never at a lower ebb, and God Himself never less honoured or worse served in Christendom*" (STOW'S *Annals*, and COLLIER'S *Ecclesiast. Hist.*, part ii. book iii. p. 218).

Bishop LATIMER, in his seventh sermon before Edward VI., said :—
"I never saw, surely, so little discipline as is nowadays. Men will be masters : they will be masters and no disciples. Alas! where is this discipline now in England? The people regard *no* discipline; they be without all order. Where they should give place, they will not stir one inch: . . . if a man say anything unto them, they regard it not. Men, the more they know, the worse they be : it is truly said 'Scientia inflat,' knowledge maketh us proud, and causeth us to forget all, and set away discipline. *Surely in Popery they had a reverence; but now we have none at all.* I never saw the like ! . . . What blasphemy do we daily commit ; what little regard have we to Christ's blessed Passion !" (*Serm.* xiii., Parker Society edit., Cambridge, 1844, p. 230).[1]

---

[1] In his " Sermon of the Plough," preached in 1548, Latimer says :—There is in London as much pride, covetousness, cruelty, oppression, and superstition as ever there was in Nebo. . . . *London was never so ill as it is now. In times past*

BERNARD GILPIN declares that in Edward's (VI.) reign, "More blind superstition, ignorance, and infidelity were promulgated in England than ever were under the Bishop of Rome. The realm was in danger of becoming more barbarous than Scythia" (*Sermons on the Crymes of the Realm*, ap. BURKE, *Historical Portraits of the Tudor Dynasty*, vol. ii. p. 296).

BRADFORD says :—"All men may see that *immorality in its foulest forms, pride, dishonesty, unmercifulness,* scoffing at religion and virtue, and a desire to oppress and crush down the poor, far surpassed at this time anything that ever before occurred in the realm" (*On the Condition of Public Morals and the People's Povertie*). And in a letter to Archbishop Cranmer, the same author says :—"A heavy curse seems to have fallen on the people ; I know not what to think of it. Desolation overshadows this land of ours, that was once so prosperous and contented" (ap. BURKE, p. 297).

STRYPE says :—"About this time the nation grew *infamous for the crime of adultery. It began among the nobility and better classes, and so spread at length among the inferior sort of people.* Noblemen would frequently put away their wives and marry others, if they liked another woman better, or were like to obtain wealth by her. And they would sometimes pretend their former wives to be false to them, and so be divorced, and marry again those whom they might fancy. . . . These adulteries and divorces increased very much ; *yea, and marrying again without any divorce at all, it became a great scandal to the realm and to the religion professed in it.* This state of morals gave much sorrow and trouble to good men to see it, insomuch that they thought necessary to move for an Act of Parliament to punish adultery with death. This Latimer, in a sermon preached in the year 1550, signified to the king : 'For the love of God, take an order for marriage here in England'" (STRYPE'S *Memorials of Cranmer*, vol. i. pp. 293, 294).

CAMDEN states that "sacrilegious avarice ravenously invaded Church livings, colleges, chantries, hospitals, and places dedicated to the poor, as things superfluous. *Ambition and emulation among the nobility, presumption and disobedience among the common people, grew so extravagant that England seemed to be in a downright frenzy*" (*Chronicle on Edward's Reign*, ap. BURKE, op. cit. p. 305).

men were full of pity and compassion ; but now there is no pity. In London their brother may lie in the streets for cold, and perish with hunger between stock and stock. I know not what to call it. In time past, when a rich man died, they were wont to help the poor scholars at the universities with exhibition : they would bequeath great sums of money to the relief of the poor. In those days they maintained Papists, and gave them livings. But now, when God's Word is brought to light, none helpeth the scholar nor the poor" . . . (ap. DIXON, *Hist. of the Church of Eng. from the Abolition of the Roman Jurisdiction*, vol. ii. 1881, p. 489).

Bishop BARLOW wrote in 1553 :—"Mark it substantially in cities and towns where ye see the people the most rifest and most busy to prate of the gospel, whether they be or be not as great usurers, deceivers of their neighbours, blasphemous swearers, evil speakers, and given to all vices as deeply as ever they were. *This I am sure of, and dare boldly affirm, that sith the time of this new contentious learning the dread of God is greatly quenched, and charitable compassion sore abated"* (*A Dialogue on the Lutheran Faccions,* 1553).

PARKHURST writes to Bullinger in 1562 :—"Religion is in the same state among us as heretofore. . . . Almost all are covetous, all love gifts. There is no truth, no liberality, no knowledge of God. Men have broken forth to curse and to lie, and murder and steal, and commit adultery," &c. (*Zurich Letters,* Parker Soc. edit., Let. xlvi.).

For copious proofs of the generally infamous character of the Protestant *clergy* in the reign of Queen Elizabeth, see Mr. BUCKLE's article in FRAZER'S MAGAZINE for August 1867. This writer remarks that "*during the whole of the sixteenth century the situation of the clergy went on degenerating;*" and that "the proofs which are extant of the *gross ignorance* of the clergy in the reign of Elizabeth are such as would stagger the most incredulous, even if they were not confirmed by every description of historical testimony that has come down to us."[1]

Present Religious Condition of Germany and England.

Much evidence on this subject has been accumulated by Mr. MARSHALL in his *Developments of Protestantism* (Richardson, 1849), and in the last chapter of his work on *Christian Missions* (2d edit., Longmans & Co.).

GERMANY.—Mr. DEWAR, English chaplain at Hamburg, writes in 1844 : —" Religious indifference has pervaded the mass of the people. It is a fact which every traveller who has visited the shores of Germany has remarked, that there is no regard for the ordinances of religion. In Hamburg and its suburbs there are five parish churches and two smaller churches. The congregation attending all the services of all these never, I am told, amount to 3000 in number, so that the remainder of the enormous population, amounting to 150,000, pays no manner of worship to their God.

---

[1] For the history of the " Reformation " in this country (which Lord MACAULAY characterises as "a mere political job, commenced by Henry, the murderer of his wives ; continued by Somerset, the murderer of his brother ; and completed by Elizabeth, the murderer of her guest "—*Essay on Hallam's Constitutional Hist.*), the reader may be referred to the admirable *Six Historical Lectures* by the late Dr. J. WATERWORTH, to vol. i. of the *Clifton Tracts,* and to Dr. F. G. LEES' *Church under Queen Elizabeth.* The early vols. also of *The History of the English Church from the Abolition of the Roman Jurisdiction,* by Canon DIXON (Protestant), and Mr. BURKE's *Historical Portraits of the Tudor Dynasty* (3 vols. 8vo), promise to exhibit the results of the latest and most exhaustive researches into the history of that event.

. . . And Hamburg in these matters does not furnish a low standard when compared with the rest of Germany. In Berlin, for instance, there is a parish which contains 54,000 inhabitants, and the annual number of communicants is 1000 less than in the largest parish of Hamburg, while the population is one-third larger " (*German Protestantism*, Oxford, 1844).

Mr. SAMUEL LAING, a Scotch Presbyterian, says :—" If the question is reduced to what really are its terms in Germany[1] at present—Catholicism, with all its superstitions, errors, and idolatry, or to no religion at all, that is to say, not avowed infidelity, but the most torpid apathy, indifference, and neglect of all religion—it may be doubted if the latter condition of a people is preferable. *The Lutheran and Calvinistic Churches in Germany and Switzerland are in reality extinct.* The sense of religion, its influence on the habits, observances, and life of the people, is *alive only in the Roman Catholic population*" (*Notes on the German Catholic Church*, Lond., 1845, p. 145). Compare the same author's *Notes of a Traveller*, 1st series, chaps. ix. and xvii.

Dr. SCHWABE writes in 1870 :—" The ancient ties of the Protestant Church are broken. Spirit and strength are lacking to replace them by new ones. At no period has the Church commanded less and given less satisfaction to man. Statistics show how far this alienation has proceeded. Of 630,000 Protestants, 11,900, viz., nearly 2 per cent., attend church on the Sundays ; and amongst them 2225 go to the Dom, merely for a musical treat. Religious indifference appears no less conspicuously in the fact that out of 23,969 interments, 3777, or nearly 15 per cent., only, are attended by religious services " (*Betrachtungen über die Volkseele*, Berlin, 1870).

The Churches provide accommodation for only 25,000 out of 800,000

---

[1] It should be observed that infidelity in foreign countries—whether Protestant or Catholic—is entirely the offspring of the English Deism of the seventeenth and eighteenth centuries. M. VILLEMAIN declares that the French philosophy of the last century owed its origin to the English writers Herbert, Hobbes, Shaftesbury, Toland, Collins, Woolston, Bolingbroke, Hume, &c., and the same may be said of the Rationalism and Pantheism of Germany. This is acknowledged by Protestant writers. Thus, the QUARTERLY REVIEW (Jan. 1861, p. 288) speaks of " our old English Deists, who were *the true fathers of French Atheism and German unbelief.*"

Dr. HAROLD BROWNE says :—" In the latter half of the eighteenth century the Deism which had been troubling England had passed through the alembic of French scepticism, and now settled down in a shower of Rationalism on Germany. The Rationalism of Paulus, the Pantheism of Hegel, the historical myth of Strauss, derive their pedigree from the writings of Lord Herbert of Cherbury, Toland, Tindal, and other English Deists, . . . through the school of Rousseau and Voltaire. . . . It was this special principle [of the English Deists] which passed through the various forms of French infidelity, German Rationalism and Pantheism, and which has been brought back to us as the highest result of modern discoveries in science and mental philosophy " (*Aids to Faith*, pp. 295, 296).

E

souls in Berlin, yet they are all but empty on Sundays (*Religous Thought in Germany*, reprinted from *Times*, 1870, p. 27).

Mr. BARING GOULD writes in 1879 :—" Throughout Germany 14 out of 100 persons attend church on Sunday ; in the town of Darmstadt only 3.3 in a hundred ; in the towns of Mainz (among the Protestants), 5.1 ; Giessen, 5.7 ; Worms, 6.3. In Darmstadt, out of 100 marriages, 34.5 per cent., in Offenbach 48.6, in Worms 44, are celebrated before the registrar alone, without religious service ; burial without religious service throughout Germany in 29.6 out of 100 inhabitants ; in Darmstadt, 60 per cent." (*Germany, Past and Present*, vol. ii. p. 164). See also the work entitled *Home Life in Germany*.

ENGLAND.—W. J. CONYBEARE, speaking of "the infidelity now so general among the best-instructed portion of the labouring classes," says :—" It is a melancholy fact that the men who make our steam-engines and railway carriages, our presses and telegraphs, the furniture of our houses and the clothing of our persons, *have now in a fearful proportion renounced all faith in Christianity*. They regard the Scripture as a forgery and religion as priestcraft, and are living without God in the world. The revelations of the late census have shown that *in England alone there are more than five millions of persons who absent themselves entirely from religious worship*" (CONYBEARE'S *Essays, Ecclesiastical and Social*, p. 99).

Canon MONEY, of Deptford, said at the Plymouth Church Congress in 1876 :—" However the sections of the working class might differ in intelligence, in sobriety, in honesty, they nearly all agreed in this—*they were alienated from Christianity. Barely five per cent. attended public worship*."

The Rev. T. HUGO added, that "*the masses of Lancashire and oj London were as heathen as those of whom St. Paul drew a picture* in immortal though dreadful colours. . . . He knew the mobs of London and Lancashire well, and he gave them his word of honour as a Christian priest, *that there was no difference between them and the people whom St. Paul portrayed*. Then, as a matter of course, they had to look at these masses *as simply heathen*" (*Church Times*, Oct. 13, 1876).

The BISHOP OF ROCHESTER, in a sermon preached in the Chapel Royal, St James's, laments "that dense, and coarse, and almost brutal ignorance, in which the toiling masses of the people who have outgrown the Church's grasp are permitted to live and die, of all that touches their salvation and explains their destiny. To hundreds of thousands of our fellow-countrymen, Almighty God is practically an unknown Being, except as the substance of a hideous oath : Jesus Christ, in His redeeming love and human sympathy, as distant as a fixed star" (*Good Words*, Jan. 1880, p. 61).

WHITAKER'S ALMANACK gives the following LIST OF PROTESTANT SECTS NOW EXISTING IN THE UNITED KINGDOM.

Advent Christians.
Advents, The.
Apostolics.
Arminian New Society.
Baptists.
Baptized Believers.
Believers in Christ.
Believers in the Divine Visitation of Joanna Southcote, Prophetess of Exeter.
Believers Meeting in the Name of the Lord Jesus Christ.
Bible Christians.
Bible Defence Association.
Brethren.
Calvinists and Welsh Calvinists.
Calvinistic Baptists.
Catholic Apostolic Church [Irvingites].
Chapels of other Wesleyans than those enumerated.
Christians Owning no Name but the Lord Jesus.
Christians who object to be otherwise designated.
Christian Believers.
Christian Brethren.
Christian Disciples.
Christian Eliasites.
Christian Israelites.
Christian Mission.
Christian Teetotallers.
Christian Temperance Men.
Christian Unionists.
Christadelphians.
Church of England.[1]
Church of Scotland.
Church of Christ.
Church of the People.
Church of Progress.
Congregational Temperance Free Church.
Countess of Huntingdon's Connection.

Covenanters.
Coventry Mission Band.
Danish Lutherans.
Disciples in Christ.
Disciples of Jesus Christ.
Eastern Orthodox Greek Church.
Eclectics.
Episcopalian Dissenters.
Evangelical Free Church.
Evangelical Mission.
Evangelical Unionists.
Followers of the Lord Jesus Christ.
Free Catholic Christian Church.
Free Christians.
Free Christian Association.
Free Church (of Scotland).
Free Church (Episcopal).
Free Church of England.
Free Evangelical Christians.
Free Grace Gospel Christians.
Free Gospel and Christian Brethren.
Free Gospel Church.
Free Gospellers.
Free Methodists.
Free Union Church.
General Baptist.
General Baptist New Connection.
German Evangelical Community.
German Lutherans.
German Roman Catholics.
Glassites.
Glory Band.
Greek Catholic.
Halifax Psychological Society.
Hallelujah Band.
Hope Mission.
Humanitarians.
Independents.
Independent Methodists.
Independent Religious Reformers.
Independent Unionists.
Inghamites.

[1] Lord MACAULAY well observed that the religion of the Church of England itself "is in fact a bundle of religious systems without number, . . . *a hundred sects battling within one Church*" (*Essay on Church and State*).

Israelites.
Latter-Day Saints.
Lutherans.
Methodist Reform Union.
Missionaries.
Modern Methodists.
Moravians.
Mormons.
Newcastle Sailors' Society.
New Church.
New Connection General Baptists.
New Connection Wesleyans.
New Jerusalem Church.
New Methodist.
Old Baptists.
Open Baptists.
Order of St. Austin, The
Orthodox Eastern Church.
Particular Baptists.
Peculiar People.
Plymouth Brethren.
Polish Society.
Portsmouth Mission.
Presbyterian Church in England.
Presbyterian Church of England.
Presbyterian Baptists.
Primitive Congregation.
Primitive Free Church.
Primitive Methodists.
Progressionists.
Protestant Members of the Church of England.
Protestants adhering to Articles 1 to 18, but rejecting Ritual.
Protestant Trinitarians.
Protestant Union.
Providence.
Quakers.
Ranters.
Rational Christians.
Reformers.
Reformed Church of England.
Reformed Episcopal Church.
Reformed Presbyterians or Covenanters.
Recreative Religionists.

Refuge Methodists.
Reform Free Church Wesleyan Methodists.
Reformed Presbyterians.
Revivalists.
Revival Band.
Salem Society.
Sandemanians.
Scottish Episcopal Church.
Scotch Baptists.
Second Advent Brethren.
Secularists.
Separatists (Protestants).
Seven-Day Baptists.
Society of the New Church.
Spiritual Church.
Spiritualists.
Strict Baptists.
Swedenborgians.
Temperance Methodists.
Testimony Congregational Church.
Trinitarians.
Union Baptists.
Union Churchmen.
Union Congregationalists.
Union Free Church.
Unionists.
Unitarians.
Unitarian Baptists.
Unitarian Christians.
United Christian Church.
United Free Methodist Church.
United Brethren or Moravians.
United Presbyterians.
Universal Christians.
Unsectarian.
Welsh Calvinistic Methodists.
Welsh Free Presbyterians.
Welsh Wesleyan Methodists.
Wesleyans.
Wesleyan Methodist Association.
Wesleyan Reformers.
Wesleyan Reform Glory Band.
Working Man's Evangelistic Mission Chapels.

www.ingramcontent.com/pod-product-compliance
Lightning Source LLC
Chambersburg PA
CBHW032044090426
42733CB00030B/647